READY-TO-GO GAME SHOWS (THAT TEACH SERIOUS STUFF)

Catholic Teachings and Practices Edition

READY-TO-GO GAME SHOWS (THAT TEACH SERIOUS STUFF)

Catholic Teachings and Practices Edition

Michael Theisen

Saint Mary's Press
Winona, Minnesota
www.smp.org

Genuine recycled paper with 10% post-consumer waste.
Printed with soy-based ink.

The publishing team included Laurie Delgatto, development editor; Cheryl Drivdahl, copy editor; James H. Gurley, production editor and typesetter; Cindi Ramm, art director; Cären Yang, designer; C. J. Potter, illustrator and cover designer; manufactured by the production services department of Saint Mary's Press.

The acknowedgments continue on page 143.

The activities in this book are not formally associated with any trademarked television game show or board game, past or present.

Printed in the United States of America

Printing: 9 8 7 6 5 4 3 2

Year: 2010 09 08 07 06 05 04 03

ISBN 0-88489-757-5

Library of Congress Cataloging-in-Publication Data

Theisen, Michael.
    Ready-to-go game shows (that teach serious stuff) : Catholic teachings and practices edition / Michael Theisen.
        p. cm.
Summary: Provides instructions for various interactive games based on popular game shows, which require minimal setup and few required materials and increase players' knowledge of Catholicism.
ISBN 0-88489-757-5 (spiral)
        1. Bible games and puzzles—Juvenile literature. 2. Christian education—Activity programs—Juvenile literature. 3. Catholic Church—Doctrines—Juvenile literature. [1. Bible games and puzzles. 2. Catholic Church—Doctrines.] I. Title.
GV1507.B5T5332002
268'.433—dc21

                                                                                                2002000225

For Jeannie Raisbeck, who does whatever is asked and so much more:
assistant, friend, and grandmother galore.
Thanks for making the last ten years of ministry such a joy.
May you never retire from what you do best!

In gratitude to my supportive and understanding wife, Mary,
who puts up with all my games,
and to Chris, David, and Rachel,
who remind me daily why it is important to keep playing!

With thanks to Brian Singer-Towns, at Saint Mary's Press,
for his advice, bad jokes, and friendship.
All were needed in the development of this series.

In thanksgiving to the Diocese of Rochester
and the staff of the Department of Evangelization and Catechesis,
for continuing to support young people,
and for encouraging the ongoing growth
of youth ministry throughout the diocese,
which makes all this work worthwhile.

GAME SHOW LISTINGS

INTRODUCTION: TRUTH OR CONSEQUENCES

Hi; we are your Ready-to-Go hosts, Francis and Clare! We congratulate you on choosing the fun and popular game ideas in this book to help your youth increase their knowledge of Catholic events, practices, and people. And what better way to show you how to use these games than by having you participate in a game yourself? As you answer the following questions, you will gain incredible insights into using this book to achieve maximum learning potential (MLP) with the young people you lead. All you need are 10 minutes of uninterrupted time, a highlighter (optional—and only if you are really into this), and a sense of humor (absolutely essential). So place yourself in a comfortable chair, turn off the phone, and let the game begin!

$1,000 Question: A stitch in time saves what?

- A. the whales
- B. seventy times seven times
- C. your pants from falling down
- D. you from repeating the same thing over and over and over again

Best response. D

Ever tried to teach someone something that you thought was really cool and they thought was NOT!? So what did you do? If you are like most of us, you said the same thing again and again, only *louder* so that they and all the neighbors could hear you. Sometimes it's not the subject matter that fails us; rather it is the way we are presenting it.

You already know that first impressions count for a lot. By using formats similar to those of popular games that are familiar to most young people, *Ready-to-Go Game Shows (That Teach Serious Stuff): Catholic Teachings and Practices Edition* creates an interactive and attention-grabbing environment that makes a great first impression. Once you have the young people's attention, half your job of teaching (usually the most difficult half) is already accomplished!

Ready-to-Go Game Shows was created so that all the shows can be done easily, with minimal setup and few required materials. They really are *ready-to-go*. All you need to do is add young people, mix, and bake with high energy, and you'll get a treat that is really something to talk about. Best of all, each show has been field-tested with both younger and older adolescents who are still alive to talk about it. If at any point you are not 100 percent satisfied with this book, then you can place it in a dark corner of your bookcase where it will make you appear to be an avid reader of a lot of interesting books with weird titles.

$10,000 Question: If you had to choose one item to take from your house before it burnt to the ground, which would you most likely select?

    A. your CD collection
    B. your jewelry collection
    C. your computer
    D. your Ready-to-Go supply box (and this book)
    Best response. D

Most of that other stuff can be replaced, but once you put together your game show supply box, you'll really believe it is the most valuable thing in the world (well, close to it anyway). After you gather the suggested items, doing any of the game shows described in this book will be 78 percent easier, leaving a mere 22 percent of the work required to achieve 100 percent MLP.

Suggested items for your Ready-to-Go supply box are these:
- a box (always a good thing to start with)
- markers
- blank paper
- pens or pencils
- a die (two dice if you are feeling really lucky!)
- tape (masking and clear)
- prizes (small items such as pencils [new or already chewed on], fast-food coupons and toys, inspirational bookmarks, leftover Halloween candy with the wrappers intact, new or slightly used toy cars)

Once you have your box all put together, keep it away from open flames and in a clean, dry place. Be sure to write in big capital letters somewhere on the box, "MY BOX." This will help deter others from thinking that it is "THEIR BOX," thereby leaving you worry free and once again, *ready-to-go.*

An Important Note About the Prize Thing

Achieving MLP is easier if these game shows are more fun than competitive. Whether the game shows are considered pure fun or do-or-die competition is under the direct control of the game show host. So you might want to make sure that everyone wins a prize or that prizes are given out at random and are all of similar value. That might mean that absolutely no prizes are awarded to anyone unless they clean up the room when the session is done. Be prepared for arguments and possible hard feelings if you decide to make these game shows more competitive than cooperative.

$100,000 Question: What happened on 31 September 1943 that changed the world?

A. the Triduum was built in Washington, D.C.

B. Thousands of cardinals were seen flocking to Rome.

C. Matthew, Mark, Luke, and John first appeared on the *Ed Sullivan Show.*

D. Nothing much ever happens on 31 September.

Best response. D

To make these game shows learning experiences, the leader must remember that the questions (and answers) serve as only the beginning of the learning experience. For example, in answering this question, some of you may have gone to the Internet to look up the date to see what *really* happened on 31 September 1943. Others may have already concluded that nothing happened because 31 September does not exist. If you were playing this game show as part of a group, I would instruct the group members to turn to their calendars to find the correct answer, leading the group to ask the obvious question, "Who hid 31 September and why?"

These game shows can be used to review Catholic material already covered in your school or parish programs, to introduce new material, or to entertain an entire school when the special speaker does not show up for the scheduled assembly. Many of the game show questions offer *tidbits*, that is, little bits of TID (terrific information drops). You can use the tidbits to help the young people learn more about the questions' topics. You can also use the tidbits to wow the audience by making it appear that you know just about everything there is to know about Catholic beliefs and practices—which is not a bad thing until you become a contestant yourself.

Another way to use the questions as a learning experience is to have the contestants, teams, or audience discuss what they know about each tidbit. This can lead to a brief discussion about the person or event or practice that the corresponding question refers to. Of course, the longer a particular discussion takes place without the benefit of food, humor, or a bad joke, the more chance there is of losing the participants' attention. Therefore the follow-up should be kept to a minimum unless the group is contained in a high-security area that is well guarded, with little or no chance of escape.

$1,000,000 Question: Who was the greatest baby-sitter of all time?

A. Pope John XXIII
B. Eve
C. Joan of Arc
D. David

Best response. D (David rocked Goliath to sleep.)

To create MLP, the host needs to be more than a baby-sitter. You need to take the risk of going beyond the directions and questions in this book and make adaptations to fit the particular needs of your group. Please allow yourself maximum flexibility with each show so that it becomes *your* show. If you have fun *leading* it, then chances are, the young people will have fun *learning* it. Here are four hot suggestions for adapting these game shows.

Start Where the Contestant Is

Try rewording questions (and sometimes even answers) to make them either easier or more challenging for your audience, as the need and knowledge level demand. For example, if a contestant is asked to name the twelve Apostles, you could make it easier by having the contestant name four, six, or eight of the Apostles. Or you could make it harder by asking the contestant to name the twelve Apostles in 30, 45, or 60 seconds. To make it impossible, you could ask the contestant to name the social security numbers of the Apostles . . . in order from the lowest to the highest.

Choose the Game That Fits Your Group

Some of the game shows were created to be easier than others. Use the game shows that best match the knowledge level of the group you are working with. The easier game shows to play are these:

- "The Real Fortune"
- "Catholic Pictionary"

The game shows that are of medium difficulty are as follows:

- "Who Wants to Be a Catholic Millionaire"
- "Faithful Feud"
- "Holy, Holy, Holy Squares"

The game shows that are a bit more challenging are these:

- "Catholic Jeopardy"
- "The Church Is Right"
- "Grace Ball"

Turn Young People into Catholic Theologians

After playing a particular game and getting a feel for the way the questions are worded, invite the young people to develop, on index cards, their own questions and answers about Catholic teachings and practices. Keep the questions in your coveted Ready-to-Go supply box and use them the next time you play the game. The more often you play the games, the better chance you have for achieving MLP.

Bridge the Generation Gap

Use the game shows as a strategy for bringing parents and young people together for an intergenerational event. Pair up parents and young people so that they have to work together as contestants. This may inspire them to read or talk about their Catholic faith more at home. Or it might just encourage them to watch reruns of television game shows to learn winning strategies for the next time they play.

$5,000,000 Question: If your best friend jumped into a swimming pool filled with a mixture of six-week-old sour milk and rotten eggs, would you do it too?

A. Yes; after all, it is my best friend.
B. It would depend on what I had just eaten.
C. It would depend on what my best friend had just eaten.
D. No. (My mother always warned me this could happen.)

Best response. D (You are probably seeing the pattern now, right?)

That's right, some things you just have to say no to. In fact, you might as well start to practice saying it: "No!" Try it again: "NO!" You may at times even have to expand on your new word with a phrase such as, "No, not now." Or try it in another language, like, "Nada" or "Nyet." Face it, once you start using *Ready-to-Go Game Shows,* you are going to have to tell the young people that there is much more to life than playing games all day long.

This may require you to train a replacement host or at least a cohost or two, who can take over the reins when you are feeling overwhelmed with your string of successful sessions using the game show approach. When you hit this "problem" (and you *will* hit this problem), why not empower a young person (or two or three) to take over for a while? Your protégés might even learn *more* by leading a show than by playing it. Then you will have gone from host extraordinaire to pure MLP genius!

Our Sponsors

Questions and answers for the game shows in this book were created using the following resources:

Ahlers, Julia, Barbara Allaire, and Carl Koch. *Growing in Christian Morality.* Rev. ed. Winona, MN: Saint Mary's Press, 1996.
Klein, Peter. *The Catholic Sourcebook.* 3d ed. [Dubuque, IA]: Harcourt Brace and Co., Brown-ROA, 2000.

Koch, Carl. *The Catholic Church: Journey, Wisdom, and Mission.* Winona, MN: Saint Mary's Press, 1994.

McBride, Alfred. "From Pentecost to Vatican II: Ten 'Peak Moments' of Church History." In *Catholic Update,* no. 0687, 1987.

McBrien, Richard P. *Catholicism.* Study ed. San Francisco: Harper and Row, Publishers, 1981.

Singer-Towns, Brian, ed. *The Catholic Youth Bible.* Winona, MN: Saint Mary's Press, 2000.

Stoutzenberger, Joseph. *Celebrating Sacraments.* Winona, MN: Saint Mary's Press, 1993.

Theisen, Michael. *Exploring Catholicism.* Winona, MN: Saint Mary's Press, 1996.

_____. *Ready-to-Go Game Shows (That Teach Serious Stuff): Bible Editon.* Winona, MN: Saint Mary's Press, 2001.

Zanzig, Thomas, et al. *Understanding Catholic Christianity.* Winona, MN: Saint Mary's Press, 1997.

A Final Word

If you are still reading this introduction, then you have gone way too far. Please stop immediately and get started playing some games. After all, they are all set and *ready-to-go!*

WHO WANTS TO BE
A CATHOLIC MILLIONAIRE

Object of the Game

This game is modeled after the popular game show *Who Wants to Be a Millionaire.* The entire group is invited to participate in a Fast Thinking preliminary round to decide who will be the lucky contestant that sits in the Nervous Kneeler's seat. The winner of the Fast Thinking round gets to try to answer five questions about the Catholic faith in order to win 1,000,000 virtues. Each final–round contestant is afforded one of two possible lifelines that can be used to help answer any one question.

HOW THE GAME IS PLAYED

Players

- [ ] one host
- [ ] contestants (who can include the entire group)

Supplies

- [ ] slips of scrap paper or index cards, and pencils for everyone
- [ ] responses for the Fast Thinking questions on pages 21–38, written on newsprint or an overhead for all to see
- [ ] a watch or clock that displays seconds
- [ ] prizes

Room Setup

Nervous Kneeler's seat → ◯

⊗ ← Host

Audience

Game Directions

1. The game show host gathers the contestants around the table, and distributes slips of paper or index cards, and pencils, to all for the Fast Thinking question. The host instructs the contestants to write their name on their paper, and the numbers 1 through 4 down the left side of the paper. Then the host tells the group that a question will be read, with four responses listed on the newsprint (or overhead). The contestants must write the responses down in the correct order as indicated by the question. Only the letter corresponding to each answer needs to be written on the paper.

2. The host reads a Fast Thinking question from the questions-and-answers section on pages 21–38. As soon as the contestants write the letters in the order that they think is correct, they stack their papers on the table in order, with the paper of the first person to finish on the bottom of the pile. After all the lists are placed on the table, the host turns the pile over and begins checking them for accuracy. The first person whose list is correct gets to sit in the Nervous Kneeler's seat for the next series of questions. All the other contestants take seats in the audience until the round is completed.

3. During the Nervous Kneeler's round, the host asks the contestant in the Nervous Kneeler's seat up to five questions, one at a time. The questions become increasingly difficult, and each has four possible answers. When the contestant is thinking through an answer, the host encourages him or her to do so out loud so that all can hear what's going on in the contestant's mind. Once the contestant has selected a final answer, the host involves the audience by asking what they would answer and why. Then the host reveals the correct answer and the tidbit information that is provided.

4. The contestants may choose *one* lifeline from the two options listed below, which they may use to help them answer any *one* of the questions. The host explains these options at the beginning of the game and determines their use during the game.

- *50/50.* The host deletes two incorrect answers, leaving the correct answer and one incorrect answer to choose from.
- *Poll the Audience.* The audience use a show of hands to indicate which answer they think is correct.

Remember, each player gets to use only *one* lifeline during his or her turn in the Nervous Kneeler's seat.

5. As soon as a player misses a question, the game is over for that player and a prize (if any) is awarded. A new round starts with the next Fast Thinking question. Everyone who has not already had a chance in the Nervous Kneeler's seat participates in the new round.

Prizes

Try to secure donations of various prizes from area businesses that are frequented by young people (such as fast-food restaurants, record stores, amusement parks, bowling alleys, and dollar stores), or use various amounts of candy as prizes. Separate the prizes into five categories: 100-, 1,000-, 10,000-, 100,000-, and 1,000,000-virtue prizes. For example, players might get one Tootsie Roll if they correctly answer the 100-virtue question, three Tootsie Rolls if they make it through the 1,000-virtue question, five Tootsie Rolls if they make it through the 10,000-virtue question, and so on.

Variations on the Game

Team play. Divide the group into teams, direct the teams each to develop five questions and possible answers (from easy to difficult) for the other team or teams, and then invite the teams to take turns hosting a show for the group.

PowerPoint presentation. If you or someone in the group has access to PowerPoint and presentation equipment, use it to display the questions and answers with a professional look.

Youth teaching younger children. Help the group take the show on the road, hosting it for younger children's groups or classes, basing the questions and answers on what the younger children are studying at the moment.

CATHOLIC MILLIONAIRE—QUESTIONS AND ANSWERS

Round One

Fast Thinking question. Put the following saints in the order they lived, starting with the earliest:

    A. Elizabeth Ann Seton   C. Peter

    B. Francis of Assisi   D. Augustine of Hippo

Answer. C, D, B, A

100-virtue question. Which of these is *not* a sacrament in the Catholic church?

    A. Confirmation

    B. Holy Orders

    C. Reconciliation (also called Penance)

    D. kneeling

Answer. D

Tidbit. Kneeling is a posture of prayer, not one of the seven Catholic sacraments.

1,000-virtue question. The stations of the cross are usually connected with which special day?

    A. Christmas   C. Immaculate Conception

    B. Good Friday   D. Crossing Sunday

Answer. B

Tidbit. The traditional stations of the cross consist of fourteen scenes or pictures highlighting the Passion of Jesus. The stations begin with Jesus being condemned to death and end with the body of Jesus being placed in the tomb. Many parishes feature a prayer experience involving the stations of the cross on Good Friday, the day that commemorates the death of Jesus.

10,000-virtue question. Which of these parts does not occur at Mass during the liturgy of the word?

    A. opening prayer   C. creed

    B. Gospel reading   D. responsorial psalm

Answer. A

Tidbit. The Mass is divided into four distinct but connected parts: the introductory rite (which includes the opening prayer), the liturgy of the word, the liturgy of the Eucharist, and the concluding rite.

100,000-virtue question. The initials *INRI* stand for what?
- A. "In God we trust"
- B. "Jesus Christ has risen"
- C. "Jesus is Lord"
- D. "Jesus of Nazareth, king of the Jews"

Answer. D

Tidbit. *INRI* is the Latin abbreviation for *Iesus Nazarenus Rex Iudaeorum,* which was written on a sign the Romans placed over Jesus on the cross, "accusing" him of impersonating a king.

1,000,000-virtue question. Which was the first ecumenical council ever held?
- A. Chalcedon
- B. Nicaea I
- C. Ephesus
- D. Lateran I

Answer. B

Tidbit. An ecumenical council is a gathering of bishops from around the world that is convened by the pope to make decisions regarding the teachings of the church. At the First Council of Nicaea, held in 325, the original Nicene Creed was developed. The current version of that creed is the only Christian creed accepted mutually by the Catholic, Orthodox, and major Protestant churches.

Round Two

Fast Thinking question. List these ministers in the order in which they are ordained or elevated, beginning with the first:
- A. bishop
- B. priest
- C. cardinal
- D. transitional deacon

Answer. D, B, A, C

100-virtue question. The sacrament that begins with water used as a symbol and includes a white garment and a candle is called what?

    A. Confirmation   C. Reconciliation (Penance)

    B. Baptism   D. bubble bath

Answer. B

Tidbit. Baptism is the first sacrament in the process of Christian initiation, followed by Confirmation and the Eucharist. The sacrament of Baptism welcomes an individual into the Christian community and the family of God.

1,000-virtue question. Which of these prayers is *not* said during the rosary?

    A. Lord's Prayer   C. Glory Be

    B. Magnificat   D. Apostles' Creed

Answer. B

Tidbit. The rosary does not include the saying or singing of the Magnificat, which Mary proclaimed during the Visitation, when she called on her cousin Elizabeth. All the other prayers mentioned, along with the Hail Mary, are prayed during the rosary.

10,000-virtue question. What does an acolyte do?

    A. assists the priest at the altar

    B. welcomes people as they enter church

    C. oversees the pastoral council

    D. proclaims the readings at Mass

Answer. A

Tidbit. An acolyte is also known as an altar server. He or she serves the priest during the Mass and carries the crucifix or candles, or both, during the procession.

100,000-virtue question. If you were participating in the second day of the Triduum, what would you be celebrating?

    A. the Immaculate Conception
    B. First Friday devotion
    C. Good Friday
    D. the Assumption

Answer. C

Tidbit. The Triduum occurs during Holy Week. It is a three-day period that begins with the evening Mass on Holy Thursday, continues through Good Friday and Holy Saturday, culminates in the Easter Vigil, and concludes with the evening prayer on Easter Sunday.

1,000,000-virtue question. If you saw someone wearing a purple cassock in a Catholic church, who would that person likely be?

    A. a bishop
    B. the pope
    C. a cardinal during an ordination
    D. a priest during Lent

Answer. A

Tidbit. A cassock is a full-length robe sometimes worn by clergy and lay assistants for ordinary use. In the Catholic church, black signifies a priest, purple a bishop, red a cardinal, and white the pope.

Round Three

Fast Thinking question. List these liturgical seasons in the order in which they occur from the beginning of the liturgical year:

A. Lent	C. Easter
B. Advent	D. Christmas

Answer. B, D, A, C

100-virtue question. Which of these is *not* a Gospel?

A. Matthew	C. Luke
B. Mark	D. Rocky

Answer. D

Tidbit. The four Gospels—Matthew, Mark, Luke, and John—were written between about A.D. 65 and 100, to tell future generations the story of Jesus' life, death, and Resurrection. We hear stories from the Gospels proclaimed at Mass during the liturgy of the word.

1,000-virtue question. What is a purificator used for?
  A. drying off individuals after their Baptism
  B. carrying the consecrated host to sick people
  C. recording the acts one must do for penance
  D. cleaning the cups and chalice used during Communion
Answer. D

Tidbit. Purificators are white linen cloths that are used by the priest and the eucharistic ministers to clean or purify the cups and sacred vessels during and after Communion.

10,000-virtue question. Who elects a new pope?
  A. a Vatican council   C. archbishops
  B. the College of Cardinals   D. the Roman curia
Answer. B

Tidbit. The College of Cardinals seclude themselves in Saint Peter's Basilica until a new pope is elected from among their group. This gathering is called a conclave.

100,000-virtue question. What was the split between the Eastern and Western churches called?
  A. the Protestant Reformation
  B. the Great Schism
  C. the Counter-Reformation
  D. the Divine Intervention
Answer. B

Tidbit. The Great Schism, or divide, between the Eastern church of Constantinople and the Western church of Rome came to a climax in 1054 when Roman leaders ceremoniously excommunicated the emperor of Constantinople and all his followers who had refused to conform to Latin usages in their churches.

1,000,000-virtue question. Which of these is *not* a category of saints?

    A. disciples   C. doctors

    B. virgins   D. pastors

Answer. A

Tidbit. The official categories given to saints are these:

- martyrs (who were killed for their faith)
- pastors (or bishops)
- apostles
- doctors (or theological writers)
- confessors (who suffered exile, torture, or imprisonment)
- virgins
- religious
- other holy men and women

Round Four

Fast Thinking question. List these books in the order in which they appear in the Bible, beginning with the first:

    A. Romans   C. Exodus

    B. Revelation   D. Luke

Answer. C, D, A, B

100-virtue question. Which of these would you *not* find in the sanctuary of a church?

    A. the presider's chair   C. the chalice

    B. the altar   D. Noah's ark

Answer. D

Tidbit. The sanctuary is the area of a church where the liturgy of the word and the liturgy of the Eucharist are celebrated by the priest. It contains the altar, pulpit, and presider's chair.

1,000-virtue question. Which of these people was *not* one of the twelve Apostles?

    A. Theopholus   C. Bartholomew

    B. James   D. Peter

Answer. A

Tidbit. Theopholus is a symbolic person to whom the author of Luke's Gospel dedicates that writing, and represents the entire group of Gentile Christians that the Gospel was aimed at.

10,000-virtue question. The term *Catholic* literally means what?

A. "holy"   C. "universal"
B. "apostolic"   D. "infallible"

Answer. C

Tidbit. The term *Catholic* (*katholikos* in Greek) means "universal" or "concerning the whole."

100,000-virtue question. What is the appropriate liturgical color for the Christmas season?

A. green   C. red
B. white   D. blue

Answer. B

Tidbit. White is the liturgical color that priests wear and is used to decorate the altar. White is used on all joyful and glorious occasions, such as Christmas, Easter, and many Marian feasts.

1,000,000-virtue question. What is a ciborium?

A. a linen cloth placed under the chalice
B. a container used to carry the Communion host outside of church
C. a container used to burn incense in during ceremonies
D. a container used to hold and carry the Communion host in the tabernacle

Answer. D

Tidbit. A ciborium often resembles a chalice except that it has a cover. A pyx (sounds like "pic") is used to carry the Communion host outside of church, such as to shut-ins or sick people.

Round Five

Fast Thinking question. Place these holy days of obligation for the United States in the order in which they occur during the liturgical year:

    A. All Saints' Day

    B. solemnity of Mary, Mother of God

    C. Immaculate Conception

    D. Assumption

Answer. C, B, D, A

100-virtue question. If you were overheard making an Act of Contrition, what would you be doing?

    A. rehearsing for the school play

    B. reading the Bible

    C. celebrating the sacrament of Reconciliation (also called Penance)

    D. practicing a magic trick

Answer. C

Tidbit. The Act of Contrition is a prayer to God that asks forgiveness for the sins one has committed.

1,000-virtue question. What do Catholics get on Ash Wednesday?

    A. a burnt candle

    B. their hands blessed with oil

    C. forty days to return all overdue library books

    D. ashes on their forehead

Answer. D

Tidbit. Ash Wednesday marks the beginning of Lent. The season of Lent lasts forty days and invites the faithful to prayer, almsgiving, and abstinence from meat on Fridays, as a way of preparing for Easter.

10,000-virtue question. In which Gospel does Jesus wash the Apostles' feet during the Last Supper?

    A. Matthew   C. Luke

    B. Mark   D. John

Answer. D

Tidbit. In John, chapter 13, Jesus washes the Apostles' feet to make the point that serving others is at the heart of being a follower of Jesus'. We celebrate that passage every Holy Thursday, during the Easter Triduum (part of Holy Week).

100,000-virtue question. The seal of the confession prevents a priest from doing what?

> A. leaving the confessional until everyone's confession has been heard
> B. telling anyone about another's confession
> C. not giving the penitent absolution after a confession
> D. hearing more than one person's confession at a time

Answer. B

Tidbit. Every priest is bound by the seal of confession, which requires him to not share a confession with anyone else.

1,000,000-virtue question. What is celebrated on the first Sunday after Pentecost each year?

> A. Trinity Sunday
> B. Christ the King Sunday
> C. Corpus Christi Sunday
> D. Epiphany

Answer. A

Tidbit. Trinity Sunday celebrates the belief of God in three persons— Father, Son, and Holy Spirit.

Round Six

Fast Thinking question. List these popes in the order in which they served, beginning with the earliest:

> A. Pius V
> B. John Paul II
> C. John XXIII
> D. John Paul I

Answer. A, C, D, B

100-virtue question. To be considered for official sainthood, a person has to first do what?

    A. Make the team.

    B. Know how to say the rosary.

    C. Give his or her pastor a Christmas present.

    D. Be dead.

Answer. D

Tidbit. Causes for sainthood cannot begin until a candidate has died. Even after causes are advanced, it usually takes many years for a candidate to reach the status of sainthood, and the candidate's proponents must follow a prescribed process of documentation, debate, and dialogue with the Vatican. The feast days for saints are celebrated on the anniversary of their death.

1,000-virtue question. What is the first prayer the congregation says together at Mass?

    A. Hail Mary   C. Apostles' Creed

    B. Lord's Prayer   D. sign of the cross

Answer. D

Tidbit. The celebrant begins and ends the Mass by leading everyone in making and praying the sign of the cross.

10,000-virtue question. If someone told you to go to the ambo, where would you go?

    A. a confessional

    B. the pulpit in the sanctuary

    C. the tabernacle

    D. the choir area

Answer. B

Tidbit. Ambo is another name for the pulpit where the lectors and celebrant proclaim the readings at Mass and where the homily is given.

100,000-virtue question. What current book contains the teachings and doctrines of the Catholic church?

    A. lectionary

    B. sacramentary

    C. *Catechism of the Catholic Church*

    D. Vulgate

Answer. C

Tidbit. The *Catechism of the Catholic Church,* published in 1994 and revised in 1997, is the reference tool for the teachings, beliefs, and doctrines on the Catholic church today.

1,000,000-virtue question. How many holy days of obligation are celebrated on days other than Sunday in the United States?

    A. ten   C. six

    B. eight   D. four

Answer. C

Tidbit. Rome lists ten holy days, but the number actually celebrated varies by country because each local bishop's conference can set its own. In the United States, six holy days are celebrated on days other than Sunday. Three of those holy days have to do with Mary: Immaculate Conception, solemnity of Mary, and Assumption of Mary. The other three are Christmas, Ascension, and All Saints' Day.

Round Seven

Fast Thinking question. List these parts of the Mass in the order in which they occur, beginning with the first:

    A. liturgy of the word   C. introductory rite

    B. concluding rite   D. liturgy of the Eucharist

Answer. C, A, D, B

100-virtue question. During the Visitation, who did Mary visit?

    A. Joseph at work

    B. the Avon lady

    C. Domino's Pizza

    D. her cousin Elizabeth

Answer. D

Tidbit. In Luke 1:39–56, Mary visits her older cousin Elizabeth, who is pregnant with John the Baptist. This event is celebrated each year on 31 May as the feast of the Visitation.

1,000-virtue question. What is a catechumen?

    A. a mythological character that was half-cat, half-human

    B. a person preparing to join the church

    C. an altar server

    D. a teacher

Answer. B

Tidbit. A catechumen is a person who is enrolled in the Rite of Christian Initiation of Adults (RCIA) and who will enter the Catholic church as a full member on Holy Saturday during the Easter Vigil. He or she spends many months preparing, studying, and praying with other catechumens in order to become Catholic.

10,000-virtue question. Which of these statements reflects the Catholic belief concerning Jesus?

    A. Jesus is more divine than human.

    B. Jesus is both fully human and fully divine.

    C. Jesus is more human than divine.

    D. Jesus is totally divine.

Answer. B

Tidbit. The biggest doctrinal controversy in the church centered on this very question and was finally resolved at the Council of Chalcedon in 451 when the council stated that Jesus Christ exists as one person in two natures—human and divine.

100,000-virtue question. What is the paschal mystery?

    A. Jesus has gone through death to life.

    B. Jesus is both human and divine.

    C. God exists as three separate persons—Father, Son, and Holy Spirit.

    D. Jesus was taken up to heaven after his Resurrection.

Answer. A

Tidbit. Paschal comes from the Greek word meaning "lamb." The paschal mystery holds that Jesus lived, died, and rose again, and that therefore death does not have the final say. It is the cornerstone of Catholic belief and faith and is symbolized in the paschal candle, which is lit at the Easter Vigil and from which baptismal candles are lit as a reminder of the faith that Catholics are all baptized into.

1,000,000-virtue question. Who was the first American-born saint?

> A. Elizabeth Ann Seton
> B. Kateri Tekakwitha
> C. John Henry Newman
> D. Katharine Drexel

Answer. A

Tidbit. Elizabeth Ann Seton was born in New York in 1774 and entered the Catholic faith at the age of thirty, after she had become a widow. She began a small school in Baltimore and eventually started a religious community, the Sisters of Charity. She was declared a saint in 1975.

Round Eight

Fast Thinking question. List these events from the life of Jesus in the order in which they occurred:

> A. Jesus appeared to the Apostles in the upper room.
> B. Peter denied Jesus three times.
> C. Jesus was found in the Temple by his parents.
> D. Jesus called the Apostles.

Answer. C, D, B, A

100-virtue question. God's loving, active presence in the world is known as what?

> A. luck
> B. good
> C. grace
> D. the makings of a great TV show

Answer. C

Tidbit. Grace is the experience of God acting in our lives and within us. It is undeserved and freely given to all as a sign of God's unconditional love for each person.

1,000-virtue question. Catholics believe that God reveals God's self through what means?
    A. the Scriptures
    B. Tradition
    C. billboards
    D. the Scriptures and Tradition
Answer. D
Tidbit. Whereas some other Christian denominations place God's revelation solely on the Scriptures, Catholics believe that God reveals God's self to humanity through both the Scriptures and Tradition, the teachings that have been handed down by the church over the centuries.

10,000-virtue question. Which of these is *not* referred to as one of the seven gifts of the Holy Spirit?
    A. understanding   C. fortitude
    B. peace   D. knowledge
Answer. B
Tidbit. The seven gifts of the Holy Spirit are wisdom, understanding, counsel, fortitude, knowledge, piety, and fear of the Lord.

100,000-virtue question. How many phases of Ordinary Time exist within the liturgical cycle?
    A. four   C. two
    B. three   D. one
Answer. C
Tidbit. Ordinary time has two phases, one in the winter between Christmas and Lent, and a longer one through the summer and fall between Easter and Advent.

1,000,000-virtue question. What is the Decalogue?

    A. a prayer said by the priest during the eucharistic prayer

    B. the Ten Commandments

    C. a prayer said during the liturgy of the hours

    D. a prayer said by the priest during the sacrament of Recon-
ciliation

Answer. B

Tidbit. The word *decalogue* means "ten words." The Ten Com-
mandments, revealed by God to Moses on Mount Sinai (Exodus
20:2–17 and Deuteronomy 5:6–21), form the basis for the great
commandment—to love God and neighbor—which all Christians are
called to live out.

Round Nine

Fast Thinking question. Place these steps of the Rite of Reconciliation in the order in which they occur, beginning with the first:

    A. confession

    B. greeting and sign of the cross

    C. Act of Contrition

    D. absolution

Answer. B, A, C, D

100-virtue question. Which of these is *not* considered a sacrament
of initiation in the Catholic church?

    A. Baptism   C. the Eucharist

    B. Confirmation   D. college football

Answer. D

Tidbit. The Catholic church celebrates seven sacraments as special
moments when God's grace is poured out to the people. These are
Baptism, the Eucharist, Confirmation, Reconciliation, Anointing of the
Sick, Holy Orders, and Matrimony. The three sacraments that initiate
an individual into the Catholic church are Baptism, the Eucharist, and
Confirmation.

1,000-virtue question. The inner sense of right and wrong that people possess is called what?

    A. a scapegoat   C. an unconscious

    B. a conscience   D. parents

Answer. B

Tidbit. A conscience helps individuals to make moral choices freely. The church asks that all Christians reflect on their conscience as well as prayer, the Scriptures, and Tradition when facing moral dilemmas.

10,000-virtue question. The Catholic Reformation began with what event?

    A. the Council of Trent

    B. the First Council of Nicaea

    C. the Second Vatican Council

    D. the Council of Chalcedon

Answer. A

Tidbit. The Council of Trent was held from 1545 through 1563. It spelled out and restored traditional Catholic faith and practices in the light of the Protestant Reformation. It also affirmed that God reveals God's self through both the Scriptures and Tradition, and that salvation comes through both faith and good works.

100,000-virtue question. What are the three theological virtues?

    A. faith, hope, and charity

    B. peace, love, and joy

    C. faith, peace, and hope

    D. justice, prudence, and fortitude

Answer. A

Tidbit. The theological virtues help us form a relationship with God, by enabling our participation in God's divine plan of goodness and grace.

1,000,000-virtue question. Who was Saint Benedict's sister?

    A. Saint Bernadette

    B. Saint Thérèse of Lisieux

    C. Saint Clare

    D. Saint Scholastica

  Answer. D

Tidbit. The twin of Saint Benedict, Scholastica, helped him teach monks and nuns how to read and write at the pair's famous monastery at Monte Cassino, built in 529.

Round Ten

Fast Thinking question. List these people in the order in which they appear in the Bible, beginning with the earliest:

    A. Paul   C. Moses

    B. Eve   D. Mary

  Answer. B, C, D, A

100-virtue question. Saint Francis of Assisi is the patron saint of what?

    A. slingshots   C. grave diggers

    B. animals   D. people named Francis

  Answer. B

Tidbit. Saint Francis of Assisi had a powerful conversion experience as an adult, renounced all his possessions and clothes, and lived simply among the poor, the sick, and the outcast. He founded the Franciscan order while his counterpart, Saint Clare, founded the Sisters of the Poor Clares.

1,000-virtue question. When is the Lord, Have Mercy said?

    A. after seeing a chicken fly

    B. after the greeting at Mass

    C. after the sign of peace at Mass

    D. before taking a test

  Answer. B

Tidbit. The Lord, Have Mercy, or Kyrie Eleison, is said or sung during the penitential rite at the beginning of Mass.

10,000-virtue question. The Jewish feast Passover is connected with which Christian celebration?

A. Pentecost	C. Palm Sunday
B. Epiphany	D. Holy Thursday

Answer. D

Tidbit. At the traditional Passover meal the night before he died, Jesus celebrated his last supper with his Apostles, creating a new Passover that we celebrate at every Eucharist and commemorate on Holy Thursday.

100,000-virtue question. How many levels of ordination are there in the Catholic church?

A. two	C. four
B. three	D. five

Answer. B

Tidbit. There are three levels of ordination: deacon, priest, and bishop. Cardinals and the pope are elevated to their status, but theirs is not an ordained role.

1,000,000-virtue question. Which of these titles is *not* given to a person as part of the canonization process?

A. *virtuous*	C. *servant of God*
B. *blessed*	D. *venerable*

Answer. A

Tidbit. The four titles given to a person going through the process of canonization are, in order of the steps taken, *servant of God, venerable, blessed,* and *saint.*

FAITHFUL FEUD

Object of the Game

Modeled after the game show *Family Feud,* this game invites teams of contestants to guess all the responses to fictitious surveys about Catholic trivia, events, and people, before they get three strikes, or misses. The opposing team may steal all the points if they correctly guess the survey responses that have not already been revealed.

HOW THE GAME IS PLAYED

Players

- ☐ one host
- ☐ an even number of teams with three or four contestants each
- ☐ one scorekeeper

Supplies

- ☐ two copies of the survey questions and responses on pages 46–57 (one for the host and one for the scorekeeper)
- ☐ an answer board (see the answer board setup instructions below), using a chalkboard or white board, an overhead projector, or newsprint
- ☐ small prizes (optional)

Room Setup

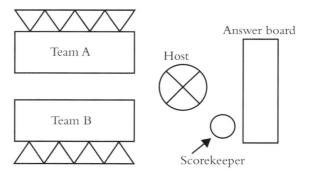

Answer Board Setup

Rank Response	Rank Response	Team Score	
1.	6.	A	B
2.	7.		
3.	8.		
4.	9.	Strikes	
5.	10.	☐ ☐ ☐	

Game Directions

1. The host divides the group into teams of three or four people. If there are more than two teams, the host chooses two to play the game, and the rest are seated as the audience (they will play later). The host identifies one of the playing teams as team A, and the other as team B.

2. The host invites one person from each playing team to step forward to compete over a toss–up question. The host reads one of the survey questions on pages 46–57. The first of the two players to yell "BEEP!" answers with a word or phrase that she or he thinks is one of the survey responses.

3. If the player's answer matches one of the responses in the list given for that question, the scorekeeper writes the word or phrase on the appropriate numbered line on the answer board and notes the appropriate points from the scoring chart on page 42. If it is not the top answer, the opposing player has the opportunity to guess a higher-ranked response.

4. The team of the player that guesses the highest-ranked response has the option to pass or play. If the team passes, the members of the opposing team try to guess all the correct responses to the toss–up question. If the team plays, its members try to guess the responses themselves.

5. The host then invites another person on the playing team to guess another response. No one is allowed to assist the person who is guessing. If someone does try to assist, the team receives a strike (an X marked on the answer board).

6. If the response the second person gives is listed on pages 46–57, the scorekeeper writes it in the correct space on the answer board. If the response is not one of the listed survey responses, the scorekeeper records a strike on the answer board.

7. Play then goes to a third person on the team. The guessing process is repeated until the team gets three strikes or correctly guesses all ten responses. If the team guesses all ten responses, it receives the maximum total of 55 points, and the round is over.

8. If the playing team gets three strikes before guessing all the responses, the opposing team has the option of stealing the points earned so far. The opposing team gets one guess at another correct response. The team members may confer with one another to determine the best guess. If their answer is on the list, they receive the total points earned by the other team plus the points for their correct answer, and the round is over. If their answer is not on the list, the playing team keeps the points it has earned, and the round is over.

9. Once a round is completed, each team sends a new person forward to play the toss-up question for the next round, and the game continues as before.

10. The game continues for a set number of rounds or a set time. Three rounds or 15 minutes makes a good game, especially if several pairs of teams need to play. The team with the highest score when the rounds are over or time is called, is declared the "Faithful Feud" winner and may be awarded a small prize. When the game is finished, the host invites two new teams up to play.

Scoring Chart

Each correct answer receives an inverted score from 1 through 10, as follows:

Survey Answer Rank	1	2	3	4	5	6	7	8	9	10
Points	10	9	8	7	6	5	4	3	2	1

Example: If all the responses are guessed, the maximum score of 55 is awarded.

Host Instructions

1. Recruit a scorekeeper ahead of time, and review with that person the process of scoring and of giving strikes for incorrect answers. Practice a round with the scorekeeper if necessary so that there is no confusion over what should be done during the actual game.

2. The survey questions have been written in such a way that they can be asked with a humorous or exaggerated emphasis. The actual responses are not the result of any scientific survey, so feel free to embellish the "authenticity" of the survey as much as you wish.

3. Consider beginning the game by reading the introductory script on pages 44–45. Then call forward your first two players and have them stand facing you. Tell them that as soon as they think they know a correct survey response, they should shout out "BEEP!" and immediately offer that response.

Variations on the Game

Team play. There are several ways to involve everyone more actively in this game:

- If your group is small enough, divide everyone into two equal teams. Let the teams each discuss possible answers as a group and respond through one player designated as their captain. After three strikes, send the play to the opposite team for its one chance at "stealing" by offering a correct answer.
- Divide the group into sets of teams (red teams A and B, blue teams A and B, et cetera) and alternate teams after each round (blue team B switches with blue team A after round 1, and so on).

Audience participation. After the teams have finished guessing and before any remaining survey responses are revealed, allow the audience to guess the remaining correct responses. Award small candy prizes for guessing a correct answer.

Real family feud. Use this game as an intergenerational event, with families and extended families competing against one another like they do in the *Family Feud* show.

INTRODUCTORY SCRIPT

To help keep the fun of this game in perspective, consider having the host use the following script to get the show, and the humor, going:

Hello, and welcome to Catholics' favorite game show, **"Faithful Feud"!** This is the show where teams get to argue about the answers to incredibly scientific surveys that have taken thousands of seconds to make up. The game is simple. Over the two-thousand-plus years that the church has been in existence, we have surveyed numerous people of relative importance, as well as numerous people with important relatives. We have used the knowledge we have gained to put together surveys and to list the top ten answers to each of the questions on them.

That's where you, our highly competitive teams, come in. Each of you will have the opportunity to test your Catholic knowledge and abilities by offering responses to these surveys, *when it is your turn* (and it's not your turn yet, so be quiet, please!).

One person from each team will be invited to come forward and stand next to me. I will ask a toss-up question. If you are one of the people called forward, as soon as you think you know a correct response, you should toss up your hand (nothing else, please) and say **"BEEP!"** Why don't we practice that now. Ready . . . **go!**

Wonderful. I'm having fun already, aren't you?! Anyway, the first person to say "BEEP!" must offer a response immediately. If the response is on the survey list, then our highly paid scorekeeper will indicate what ranking and score it gets. If it is not the number 1 response, then the opposing player gets one guess to try to top it. The player with the highest-ranked response gets to decide whether her or his team will pass (to the other team) or play the round itself.

The team playing the round will take turns guessing a response. When you are correct, you'll hear this: "You're correct." If you are wrong, you will hear this: "   ." That was the sound of *nothing.* And while you are listening to that sound, you will see our highly paid scorekeeper place an X on the board. Get three Xs, and the other team gets a chance to *steal* the win by guessing one of the remaining responses with one try. If it correctly guesses any of the remaining responses, its members will be thought of as pretty smart! Not only that, but they will win all the points that have been amassed by your team (which is pretty unfair, if you ask me). However, if their one guess is not on the survey list, your team receives the point total, and all is well in the world again.

The winning team will be the one with the most points when time expires or I expire, whichever comes first.

Now that you are totally confused, are you ready to be faithful? Then let's play **"Faithful Feud"**!

FAITHFUL FEUD—SURVEY QUESTIONS AND RESPONSES

I. A group of five thousand liturgists separating palms for Palm Sunday were asked, "What is your favorite feast or holy day?"

Rank   *Answer*

1.   Easter (marks the holiest day of the year for the Christian church, commemorating Jesus' Resurrection from the dead)

2.   Christmas (celebrates the birth of Jesus and is preceded by the season Advent)

3.   Immaculate Conception (celebrates Mary's being conceived without sin)

4.   Good Friday (commemorates the death of Jesus and usually features the stations of the cross)

5.   Pentecost (celebrates the "birthday of the church," when the Holy Spirit descended on the disciples, inspiring them to preach the Good News of Jesus Christ to the world; occurs approximately fifty days after Easter)

6.   Assumption (celebrates Mary's being assumed into heaven, body and soul)

7.   Ash Wednesday (marks the beginning of the season Lent; the palms from the previous year's Palm Sunday are used to make ashes that mark the forehead of the faithful)

8.   Palm Sunday (begins Holy Week and commemorates Jesus' triumphant welcome into Jerusalem by the very crowd that would call for his death later that week)

9.   Epiphany (is celebrated the Sunday after 1 January and commemorates the journey of the three Wise Men to find the infant Jesus in his stable; literally means "manifestation" —in this case, of God on earth)

Permission to reproduce this page for program use is granted.

10.   Christ the King Sunday (celebrates the kingship of Jesus and concludes the Catholic church's liturgical year)

2. Last year, on 1 November, during the All Saints' Convention, the top ten saints of all time were inducted into the Halo Hall of Fame. Who were they?

Rank   Answer
1.   Mary (mother of God)
2.   Joseph (Mary's husband)
3.   Francis of Assisi (founder of the Franciscan order)
4.   Elizabeth Ann Seton (first American-born saint)
5.   Thérèse of Lisieux (nun known as the Little Flower)
6.   Nicholas (saint popularized into the legendary Santa Claus)
7.   Patrick (monk who converted many in Ireland, where he had once been held as a slave)
8.   Anthony of Padua (powerful preacher in Italy and "finder of lost things")
9.   Augustine of Hippo (saint who converted from a wild lifestyle to become a great teacher and leader of the church)
10.   Clare (coworker of Saint Francis's and founder of the Poor Clares)

3. One hundred people (thirty-six priests, seven sisters, three deacons, five bishops, one cardinal, and forty-eight laypeople) were asked, "What's your favorite part of the Mass?"

Rank   Answer
1.   Communion rite (includes the Lord's Prayer, sign of peace, Lamb of God, distribution of Communion, Communion song, and prayer)

2. Gospel (is proclaimed by the priest or deacon after the second reading)
3. homily (is presented by the celebrant; breaks open the word of God and relates it to the life of the faithful)
4. entrance song (is sung during the entrance procession)
5. Gloria (is sung or recited after the opening prayer, except during the season Lent)
6. preparation of the gifts (includes the preparation of the altar, collection, presentation of the gifts, and a song)
7. eucharistic prayer (includes the preface; Holy, Holy, Holy; invocation; memorial acclamation; prayer of remembrance; Final Doxology; and Great Amen)
8. dismissal and recessional song (concludes the Mass)
9. responsorial psalm (is sung or proclaimed; is taken from the Book of Psalms and is placed between the first and second readings)
10. general intercessions (are also known as prayers of the faithful, to which the people offer a response such as, "Lord, hear our prayer")

4. Thousands of high school sophomores who read the Bible were asked, "What is your favorite book of the Bible?"

Rank Answer
1. Matthew (one of the three synoptic Gospels; was written for Jewish Christians around A.D. 85)
2. Genesis (first book of the Old Testament; contains the Creation stories as well as stories of the Hebrew patriarchs and matriarchs)

3.   Romans (first of the letters, or epistles, found in the New Testament; was written by the Apostle Paul to Jewish and Gentile Christians in A.D. 56–58)

4.   Exodus (Old Testament book; details the life of Moses and the stories of the Hebrews' great Exodus from Egypt and the slavery of Pharaoh)

5.   Psalms (150 prayers of joy, lament, praise, and thanksgiving that are sung at Mass during the responsorial psalm)

6.   Isaiah (one of the major prophetic books of the Old Testament; was actually written by three different people over the course of nearly 250 years)

7.   John (last of the Gospels to be written, most likely from A.D. 90 through 100; was aimed at all Christians, many of whom were experiencing persecution because of their faith in Jesus)

8.   Revelation (last book in the Bible; was probably written in A.D. 92–96; used the apocalyptic form of literature to offer hope to Christians in Asia Minor; despite some public opinion to the contrary, does not predict the future)

9.   Acts of the Apostles (actually written as a second part of the Gospel of Luke; tells about the early church after Jesus' Resurrection)

10. Corinthians (two letters written by Paul in A.D. 56–57 to the Gentile church at Corinth, encouraging them to be more faithful in following Christ)

5. One thousand confirmands were asked to name an important sacramental symbol.

Rank	Answer
1.	water (Water is used in Baptism to remind us of the new life all are baptized into.)
2.	oil (Chrism, or consecrated oil, is used to anoint the faithful into the living and active faith modeled for us by Jesus Christ. It is used at Baptism, Confirmation, Holy Orders, and Anointing of the Sick.)
3.	bread (During the eucharistic prayer, the bread is blessed and consecrated into the body of Christ.)
4.	wine (During the eucharistic prayer, the wine is blessed and consecrated into the blood of Christ.)
5.	wedding ring (A wedding ring is exchanged by a couple during the sacrament of Matrimony as a symbol of their pledge to love, cherish, and honor each other all the days of their lives.)
6.	white garment (A white garment is placed on the newly baptized to symbolize her or his becoming a new creation through Christ.)
7.	candle (A candle lit from the paschal candle at Baptism symbolizes the sponsors' duty to help the newly baptized always keep the light of faith burning brightly in her or his life.)
8.	laying on of hands (The laying on of hands is a symbolic gesture that occurs during the Rites of Confirmation, Ordination, and Anointing of the Sick.)
9.	absolution and imposition of hands (After hearing an individual confession during the sacrament of Reconciliation, the priest imposes his hands over the penitent and says a prayer absolving the person from her or his sins. This absolution is made possible by Jesus' death and Resurrection.)

10. people gathered (Often overlooked as a symbol of the sacraments, the faithful who are gathered to witness or participate in a sacrament testify that Catholic faith is a communal experience that must be celebrated, witnessed, and supported by others.)

6. On the first day of the new school year, ten thousand Catholic school students were asked, "What is your favorite prayer?"

Rank   *Answer*
1. Lord's Prayer (also known as the Our Father; prayer taught to the Apostles by Jesus when they asked him how they should pray)
2. Hail Mary (prayer to Mary based in part on the angel Gabriel's greeting to her when she was told that she had been chosen to bear God's Son)
3. Nicene Creed (prayer summarizing our beliefs as Christians; said at Mass after the homily as a reminder of our central, or core, beliefs; developed at the First Council of Nicaea in A.D. 325 and accepted by Catholic, Orthodox, and most major Protestant churches)
4. Glory Be to the Father (referred to as the Lesser Doxology; said at the end of psalms during the liturgy of the hours and used in the rosary and as a common conclusion to group prayers)
5. Holy, Holy, Holy (often sung at the beginning of the eucharistic prayer at Mass; based on two Scripture passages, Isaiah 6:3 and Mark 11:9–10, the latter being about Jesus' triumphant entry into Jerusalem)
6. litanies (prayers made up of a series of petitions offered by the leader and responses said by the faithful, such as: "Saint Francis . . . Pray for us")

7.   rosary (widely known form of traditional Catholic prayer; helps the pray-er focus on the four sets of mysteries that recount special moments in the life of Christ; utilizes the sign of the cross, Apostles' Creed, Hail Mary, Lord's Prayer, and Glory Be)

8.   Act of Contrition (prayer said by the penitent during the sacrament of Reconciliation as a means of noting her or his awareness of sinful actions and asking God's forgiveness for those sins)

9.   Gloria (known as the Greater Doxology; usually sung or said at Mass after the Kyrie Eleison; based on Luke 2:14, in the story of Jesus' birth)

10. Lamb of God (prayer sung or said during the breaking of the bread in the Communion rite at Mass)

7. Twelve thousand sacristans (people in charge of the sacred articles and vestments), waiting to be taught how to get candle wax out of the carpet, were asked, "What are the top ten things seen inside a Catholic church?"

Rank   Answer

1.   crucifix (Catholic churches feature crucifixes instead of just empty crosses. These are used in the processional and recessional.)

2.   chalice (The chalice holds the wine that is transformed into the blood of Christ during Mass.)

3.   altar (The altar is the central focus at Mass, serving as the table around which all the faithful are gathered to remember Jesus broken and poured out.)

4.   statues (Statues are common in many Catholic churches, often depicting Mary and Joseph at the side altars, or other famous figures from the Catholic faith tradition.)

5. paschal candle (The paschal candle stands on the altar or next to the baptismal font. It reminds us of the life, death, and Resurrection of Jesus, and all baptismal candles are lit from it. It is put away during the season Lent and is brought forth during the processional at the Easter Vigil on Holy Saturday when the catechumens are brought into the church.)

6. people (The church would be just a building without the people gathered to worship and celebrate their faith. The Second Vatican Council helped Catholics understand that they, in fact, are the living church and have a responsibility to reach out beyond the four walls of the church building to live their faith.)

7. stations of the cross (The stations of the cross consist of fourteen scenes from the trial and death of Jesus. Many churches have these placed around the inside walls or outside grounds, in the order the events happened, and use them to pray the stations on Good Friday.)

8. baptismal font (Individuals are brought to the baptismal font to be baptized into the faith. Many churches place this font in a prominent location to serve as a constant re-minder to the entire community of the faith each member has been initiated into.)

9. tabernacle (A tabernacle holds the consecrated host that is left over after Communion. Many churches place their tabernacle in a separate worship area, away from the main altar, so that people can go there to pray and reflect with-out noise or disruption.)

10. lectionary (The lectionary is the book that the lectors read from at Mass. It contains all the readings for every Sunday of the year as well as for daily Masses and feast days.)

8. Two thousand women with Mary appearing somewhere in their name were asked, "What are the top liturgical feasts involving Mary?"

Rank   Answer

1.   Immaculate Conception (The feast of the Immaculate Conception celebrates Mary's being conceived without sin. It is held on 8 December.)

2.   Birth of Mary (Mary's conception is celebrated on 8 December; her birth is celebrated exactly nine months later, on 8 September.)

3.   Presentation of Mary (It was customary for Jewish parents to bring their child to the Temple for a blessing. The presentation of Mary is celebrated on 21 November.)

4.   Christmas (The birth of Jesus in a stable in Bethlehem is celebrated on 25 December.)

5.   Holy Family (The feast of the Holy Family is celebrated on the Sunday following Christmas, and commemorates Jesus, Mary, and Joseph.)

6.   Mary, Mother of God (The solemnity of Mary, Mother of God is the oldest and most important feast commemorating Mary. It occurs exactly one week after Christmas, on 1 January.)

7.   Annunciation (The feast of the Annunciation celebrates Mary's conception of Jesus with the Holy Spirit. It is celebrated nine months before the birth of Jesus, on 25 March.)

8.   Presentation of the Lord (Forty days after the birth of Jesus, on 2 February, the church celebrates his presentation in the Temple by Mary and Joseph.)

9.   Visitation (On 31 May, the church celebrates Mary's visit to her older cousin Elizabeth, who was pregnant with John

the Baptist. During the Visitation, Mary prayed the prayer that has become known as the Magnificat.)

10.   Assumption (Celebrated on 15 August, the feast of the Assumption commemorates Mary's being assumed into heaven, body and soul.)

9. One hundred twenty people wearing red hats and standing in Saint Peter's Square were asked, "What are the things most associated with a pope?"

Rank   Answer
1.   College of Cardinals (Also known as the Sacred College, this group of cardinals is responsible for electing a new pope from within its membership. Only cardinals under the age of eighty are eligible to become pope, and the college can have no more than 120 eligible members.)
2.   Saint Peter's Basilica (Saint Peter's Basilica is one of the largest church buildings in the Christian world, covering about 4 acres. It is where the pope celebrates Mass and where a new pope is elected.)
3.   bishop of Rome (The pope is also the bishop of Rome.)
4.   encyclical (An encyclical is a letter from the pope addressed to the universal church.)
5.   Vatican (The Vatican is the pope's palace and living area.)
6.   infallibility (Infallibility is the gift from the Holy Spirit to the church that enables the pope and bishops in union with him to proclaim without error a doctrine of faith or morals.)
7.   World Youth Day (World Youth Day was begun in 1985 by Pope John Paul II and is held every other year. It gathers youths and young adults from around the world together in

faith for a week of prayer, catechesis, worship, and community building.)

8. conclave (A conclave is a meeting of the College of Cardinals in the Sistine Chapel to elect a new pope.)

9. papal ring (The papal ring, given to the pope at his election, contains the figure of Saint Peter fishing. It is officially used for sealing documents and is ceremoniously broken at the death of the pope.)

10. Peter's Pence (Peter's Pence is an annual collection taken up around the world to help pay for the pope's travel and the administration of the Holy See, the administrative and governing body of the Vatican.)

10. Two million lay ministers around the world were asked to name the top ten leadership positions within the Catholic church.

Rank   Answer

1. pope (bishop of Rome and leader of the Catholic church)
2. cardinal (leader who has been elevated from the rank of a bishop and joins other cardinals to elect the next pope)
3. bishop (ordinary, or leader, of a diocese)
4. priest (ordained man of word and sacrament)
5. deacon (ordained man who can administer some of the sacraments, such as Baptism and Matrimony. Permanent deacons may be married; transitional deacons may not because their ordination is a step toward priestly ordination.)
6. religious (men and women who take vows of poverty, chastity, and obedience; live in religious communities; and are referred to as sister or brother)
7. youth minister (lay, professed, or ordained person who ministers to and with young people in a parish or school community)

8. director of religious education (lay, professed, or ordained person who directs the catechetical aspects of a parish, including religious education, sacramental preparation, and adult education)

9. pastoral council member (lay volunteer in a parish, usually elected from among the parishioners, who advises the pastor in matters affecting the parish)

10. lay minister (person who is not ordained or professed, and who serves the faithful as a professional or volunteer within the parish or diocese)

CATHOLIC JEOPARDY

Object of the Game

Modeled after the popular game show *Jeopardy,* this game challenges contestants to answer questions in different categories of Catholic facts, teachings, and church history. The answers must be stated in the form of a question. As the questions get harder, they are worth more points for the person who answers them correctly.

HOW THE GAME IS PLAYED

Players

☐ one host
☐ three contestants
☐ one scorekeeper

Supplies

☐ a game board (see the game board setup instructions on page 60)
☐ a watch or clock that displays seconds
☐ prizes (optional)

Room Setup

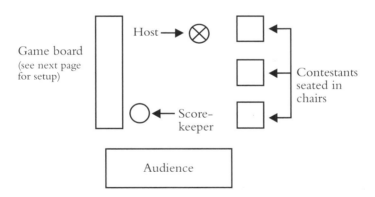

Game Board Setup

Create the following game board, using a chalkboard or white board, an overhead projector, or newsprint.

Category A	Category B	Category C	Category D
100	100	100	100
200	200	200	200
300	300	300	300
400	400	400	400
500	500	500	500

Score

Contestant 1: _____

Contestant 2: _____

Contestant 3: _____

Game Directions

1. The host selects four categories from those given in the answers-and-questions section on pages 62–71, and writes each category above a points column on the game board. Then the host selects three contestants and introduces them to the audience. Each contestant is seated in a chair.

2. The shortest contestant goes first. He or she chooses any category and point amount on the board. The host refers to the answers-and-questions section on pages 62–71 and reads the answer that corresponds to the chosen category and point amount. The contestant has 10 seconds to respond *in the form of a question.*

3. If the contestant responds correctly, the host declares the points won, and the scorekeeper crosses them off the points column and adds them to the contestant's score. Whenever a correct response is given, the host shares the background tidbit to it.

4. If the response is incorrect or there is no response within 10 seconds, the question is up for grabs to the other two contestants. As soon as the host says a question is up for grabs, the *first person to stand*

up gets to respond to it. If the response is correct, the points are added to the contestant's score; if the response is incorrect, the points are deducted from the contestant's score, and the remaining contestant has an opportunity to respond to the question. If no one gives the correct response, the host reveals the correct response and shares the tidbit, and the scorekeeper crosses the points off the game board without awarding them to any contestant.

5. The game then proceeds with the contestant to the right of the contestant who had the first chance at the previous question. No one loses a turn when a question goes up for grabs.

6. The game continues until all the points on the game board have been crossed off or until time expires. The contestant with the most points at the end wins the game. The host announces the winner and awards prizes, if they are being used.

Prizes

Prizes can be awarded to first, second, and third place, or one large prize can be given to the winner and two smaller ones to the other contestants. When selecting and awarding prizes, please remember that the emphasis is on learning Catholic facts and information and having fun, not on competition and prizes.

Variations on the Game

Team or family play. Divide the group into three teams, or have three families (or parent–child teams) play. From each team, select a captain to be the official spokesperson.

Group play. Invite everyone in the group to play, by having each person select a category and amount and attempt to answer a question. Give each member of the group a turn.

CATHOLIC JEOPARDY—ANSWERS AND QUESTIONS

Category: Inside the Church

100 points. The box where the consecrated host is kept.

Correct question. What is the tabernacle?

Tidbit. The tabernacle holds the Blessed Sacrament (consecrated host) that is not consumed during Mass. In many churches, the tabernacle is placed in a separate worship chapel or space so that people can go there to pray and meditate in quiet.

200 points. Candles that you might have to pay to light and that are usually found on side altars.

Correct question. What are votive candles?

Tidbit. Votive candles, also known as vigil lights, can often be found along side altars at the base of statues of Mary or Joseph or other key figures from the Catholic Tradition. Some churches request a small donation when they are lit, which is then used to help fund the work of the church. Often the person lighting the candle offers a prayer for a particular intention.

300 points. The book that contains the readings for the Mass and is usually placed on the ambo.

Correct question. What is the lectionary?

Tidbit. The lectionary is the book that contains all the readings for the Sunday and weekday Masses, feast days, and holy days. Lectors proclaim those readings from the ambo (the podium often found to the left of the altar).

400 points. The vestment that marks deacons and priests, and is worn in two different ways to let you know which is which.

Correct question. What is a stole?

Tidbit. A stole is a long, thin piece of fabric that goes over the alb (white robe) and hangs around the neck and down the front. Deacons wear their stole across their body at an angle, and priests wear their stole vertically.

500 points. The part of the church where the altar is located.

Correct question. What is the sanctuary?

Tidbit. The sanctuary is the part of the church where the altar, ambo, presider's chair, and sanctuary lamps or candles are found. It is the central sacred place where the bread and wine are consecrated and where the word of God is proclaimed.

Category: Pray It!

100 points. A famous prayer that begins "Lord, make me an instrument of your peace."

Correct question. What is the Prayer of Saint Francis?

Tidbit. The Prayer of Saint Francis is attributed to Francis of Assisi (1182–1229), a well-known Catholic saint who gave up a life of wealth and status to serve the sick and destitute people of his area. He began the Franciscan order.

200 points. Perhaps the most widely said prayer in the world, coming after the Great Amen at Mass.

Correct question. What is the Lord's Prayer?

Tidbit. The Lord's Prayer, or Our Father, is taken from the prayer Jesus taught to his followers when they asked him to teach them how to pray.

300 points. The prayer that a priest usually hears before absolution.

Correct question. What is the Act of Contrition?

Tidbit. The Act of Contrition is a prayer said by the penitent during the sacrament of Reconciliation. It expresses sorrow for the sins committed and a promise or intention to God to try to change the behavior and actions that led to those sins.

400 points. The prayer form that features a monstrance, the Blessed Sacrament, and a blessing of the people gathered.

Correct question. What is the Benediction?

Tidbit. The Benediction is a popular devotion of the Blessed Sacrament, in which a consecrated host is placed inside a crosslike structure called a monstrance. Various prayers are said, culminating in a procession of the monstrance and a blessing of the people gathered.

500 points. The popular prayer form that is completed in five decades.

Correct question. What is the rosary?

Tidbit. The rosary is a prayer form that uses five sets of ten beads (referred to as decades) to help a person focus on various highlights from the life of Jesus. Over fifty Hail Mary's are said through the use of this prayer form.

Category: The Liturgical Year

100 points. A forty-day period of preparation that you must go through before you can celebrate Easter.

Correct question. What is Lent?

Tidbit. Lent begins on Ash Wednesday and concludes during Holy Week. It invites the faithful to enter a period of penance, fasting, abstinence from meat on Fridays, and works of mercy, to prepare themselves for the most holy event of the year—Easter.

200 points. The season whose first Sunday marks a new year in the church.

Correct question. What is the season Advent?

Tidbit. The season Advent, which lasts four weeks and leads into the season Christmas, begins a new liturgical year in the church. Churches use an Advent wreath to mark the four Sundays that prepare the faithful for the celebration of Christ's birth.

300 points. "The birthday of the church," occurring approximately fifty days after Easter.

Correct question. What is Pentecost?

Tidbit. The feast of Pentecost (*pente* meaning "fifty") celebrates the Holy Spirit's coming upon the disciples and inspiring them to go out, despite their fears, and proclaim the Good News of Jesus Christ to every nation.

400 points. The longest liturgical season, known by the wearing of the green.

Correct question. What is Ordinary Time?

Tidbit. The liturgical color worn by priests and deacons during Ordinary Time is green. Ordinary Time has two parts. The first is celebrated after Christmas until the beginning of Lent. The second, and longest, follows Easter and lasts until Christ the King Sunday, which marks the end of the liturgical year.

500 points. The holy days that make up the Triduum.

Correct question. What is the three-day period that begins with the evening Mass on Holy Thursday, continues through Good Friday and Holy Saturday, culminates in the Easter Vigil, and concludes with the evening prayer on Easter Sunday?

Tidbit. The Triduum occurs during Holy Week and helps the faithful prepare for the celebration of Easter by recounting the last days of Jesus' life, his death, and his entombment.

Category: Saints Alive!

100 points. The process you have to go through if you want to be considered a saint in the Catholic church.

Correct question. What is canonization?

Tidbit. Canonization has three steps to it, each one requiring much dialogue, prayer, and time. If the candidate's case is accepted by Rome, that person is referred to as a *servant of God.* In the first step of the process, if the candidate's case is approved to go further, the person is referred to as *venerable.* In the second step, the candidate's life's works are carefully examined, and if they are accepted, the person is beatified and given the title *blessed.* In the third step, two miracles must be credited to the candidate's intercession with God. After these are documented, the person is canonized by the pope as an official *saint* of the Catholic church and assigned a feast day (usually the date of the person's death).

200 points. The woman who ranks number 1 when it comes to the saints (and churches named after her).

Correct question. Who is Mary?

Tidbit. Mary, the mother of God, is the most recognized saint in the Catholic church. Many churches throughout the world are named in honor of her.

300 points. The saint you pray to if something's lost.

Correct question. Who is Saint Anthony?

Tidbit. Saint Anthony is known as the saint of lost items, and is often prayed to for help in finding things.

400 points. The feast day that lets the church celebrate the saints as a group.

Correct question. What is All Saints' Day?

Tidbit. All Saints' Day is held on 1 November and is a time when the church recognizes the special place and role that the more than five thousand saints play in the people's faith and lives.

500 points. The first American-born saint.

Correct question. Who was Saint Elizabeth Ann Seton?

Tidbit. Elizabeth was a convert to the Catholic faith and worked tirelessly to help educate and care for orphans and destitute people. Pope Paul VI canonized her in 1975.

Category: A Woman to Remember

100 points. The angel that Mary said yes to when she made room for Jesus.

Correct question. Who was the angel Gabriel?

Tidbit. Mary's visitation by the angel Gabriel is celebrated through the feast of the Annunciation and is the first of the joyful mysteries prayed with the rosary.

200 points. The elderly cousin whose visit from Mary was a moving experience for both.

Correct question. Who was Elizabeth?

Tidbit. Mary went to visit Elizabeth after the angel Gabriel visited Mary. As she saw the pregnant Elizabeth, whose child would be John the Baptist, the child leaped in Elizabeth's womb and Elizabeth was "filled with the Holy Spirit" (Luke 1:41). At that point, Elizabeth proclaimed the great words we pray in the Hail Mary, "Blessed are you among women and blessed is the fruit of your womb" (verse 42).

300 points. The oldest and most important feast day of Mary, and the celebration that always starts the New Year on the right note.

Correct question. What is the solemnity of Mary, Mother of God?

Tidbit. The solemnity of Mary is celebrated on 1 January each year. Fourteen masses during the church year honor Mary.

400 points. The month that is set aside to commemorate the rosary, like May is considered the month to honor Mary.

Correct question. What is October?

Tidbit. October is the month when the church celebrates and highlights the rosary, which contains seven prayer steps: *(1)* the sign of the cross and the Apostles' Creed, *(2)* the Lord's Prayer, *(3)* three Hail Marys, *(4)* the Glory Be to the Father, *(5)* an announcement of the mystery being prayed for, followed by the Lord's Prayer, *(6)* ten Hail Marys, and *(7)* the Glory Be to the Father. The last three steps are then repeated as another mystery is meditated on.

500 points. Mary's song, which she sang during the Visitation.

Correct question. What is the Magnificat?

Tidbit. The Magnificat is found in Luke 1:46–55. Mary proclaimed this great prayer as a testimony to her faith when she met her cousin Elizabeth. It is used by the church during evening prayer.

Category: Church History

100 points. The man who began a reformation that was later countered by the Catholic church.

Correct question. Who was Martin Luther?

Tidbit. In 1517, Martin Luther posted his Ninety-five Theses, outlining abuses he saw in the church, especially regarding the sale of indulgences. This precipitated the beginning of the Protestant Reformation, which eventually resulted in the Catholic Counter-Reformation and the Council of Trent.

200 points. The great split that separated the Eastern church from the Western church.

Correct question. What was the Great Schism?

Tidbit. After hundreds of years of tension, the Eastern (Orthodox) church and Western (Roman) church split from each other in 1054.

300 points. The council opened by Pope John XXIII.

Correct question. What was Vatican Council II?

Tidbit. Pope John XXIII surprised many people by convening the Second Vatican Council in 1962. This council dramatically changed the way Catholics understood and celebrated the Mass, and ushered in a new understanding of what it means to be church in the modern world.

400 points. The men who were the first leaders of the church.

Correct question. Who were Peter and Paul?

Tidbit. Peter, the most well known of the Apostles, and Paul, the most well known convert of his day, became the first leaders of the early church after Pentecost, and helped spread to the Gentiles the Good News of God's salvation in Jesus Christ. Peter is considered the first pope of the church, although he was never given that particular title.

500 points. The man of Milan who won the church's freedom in 313.

Correct question. Who was Emperor Constantine?

Tidbit. Emperor Constantine ended the persecution of the Christians when he saw a vision of Christ before a battle with Maxentius, whom he defeated. Afterward Constantine proclaimed the Edict of Milan, which allowed Christians to celebrate their faith freely in public, something that had been impossible to do before that time. Later in life, Constantine converted to Christianity, and Christianity became the favored religion of the land.

Category: Parts of the Mass

100 points. The portion of the Mass that is responsible for getting the word out.

Correct question. What is the liturgy of the word?

Tidbit. The liturgy of the word begins after the introductory rite and includes the four readings that are proclaimed on Sunday (the first reading, psalm response, second reading, and Gospel) as well as the homily.

200 points. The liturgical season during which you'll hear no Gloria or Alleluia.

Correct question. What is Lent?

Tidbit. Lent is the forty days of preparation, fasting, and penitence that lead up to Easter. During Lent, the Gloria and the Gospel Alleluia are not said or sung, in keeping with the tone of the season.

300 points. The last part of the liturgy.

Correct question. What is the concluding rite?

Tidbit. The concluding rite begins after Communion and includes the final blessing and dismissal by the priest, followed by the closing song.

400 points. The Sunday reading during which the Old Testament is heard.

> *Correct question.* What is the first reading?

> *Tidbit.* A passage from the Old Testament is proclaimed during the first reading. At a Sunday liturgy, a passage from a New Testament book other than the Gospels is proclaimed during the second reading. A passage from one of the four Gospels (Matthew, Mark, Luke, or John) is proclaimed during the Gospel reading.

500 points. The priest's prayer book during Mass.

> *Correct question.* What is the sacramentary?

> *Tidbit.* The sacramentary contains the various prayers offered by the priest throughout the liturgy. The lectionary contains the various Scripture readings proclaimed during Mass.

Category: The Bible

100 points. The sequel to Luke, telling the story of the early church.

> *Correct question.* What is the Acts of the Apostles?

> *Tidbit.* The Book of Acts was written by Luke, who wrote the Gospel of Luke and the Acts of the Apostles as a two-volume set. Acts tells the story of the early church after Jesus' Resurrection. It was written around A.D. 80–85.

200 points. The book that is the same whether you sing it, say it, or pray it.

> *Correct question.* What is the Book of Psalms?

> *Tidbit.* There are 150 Psalms, which are grouped into five categories: hymns of praise, hymns of lament, hymns of wisdom, hymns of worship, and historical psalms. Many were attributed to King David even though most were written after his death.

300 points. The book that leads the reader through burning bushes, plagues, parted waters, dry deserts, and even some stone writing.

Correct question. What is the Book of Exodus?

Tidbit. Exodus is the story of Israel's liberation from the slavery of Pharaoh to the freedom of a covenant with God. God reveals himself as a burning bush to a prophet named Moses, who eventually leads God's people to freedom.

400 points. The Gospel you read if you want the shortest account of Jesus' life, death, and Resurrection.

Correct question. What is the Gospel of Mark?

Tidbit. Mark was the first Gospel written, in about A.D. 65–70, by a Gentile Christian trying to tell the story of Jesus to a group of non-Jewish Christians experiencing persecution for their belief in Jesus. It is a "short and sweet" Gospel portraying Jesus as a man of action who calls people into discipleship.

500 points. The last book of the Bible, revealing not the future, but rather the persecutions of a young church.

Correct question. What is the Book of Revelation?

Tidbit. Revelation is referred to as apocalyptic literature, that is, literature that uses symbolic, coded language to communicate a message of hope to a persecuted people. Revelation was written around A.D. 92–96 to Christians persecuted by the Roman emperor Domitian. The coded language allowed Christians to understand its message of God's victory over "evil" (that is, the Romans).

HOLY, HOLY, HOLY SQUARES

Object of the Game

This game show activity is modeled after that perennial favorite *Hollywood Squares*. Like in the game ticktacktoe, contestants attempt to be the first player to get three Xs or Os in a row. The three Xs or Os can be horizontal, vertical, or diagonal. Players earn the right to get their X or O on a particular square by accurately deciding whether the guest star in that square has answered a question correctly.

HOW THE GAME IS PLAYED

Players

- [ ] one host
- [ ] nine guest stars (see the section "Variations on the Game" if you cannot recruit that many guest stars from within the group)
- [ ] two contestants

Supplies

- [ ] nine blank name tags made from poster board, and safety pins or tape
- [ ] a marker
- [ ] eleven blank sheets of paper
- [ ] masking tape
- [ ] nine copies of the questions and answers for guest stars on pages 84–86
- [ ] a coin
- [ ] prizes (optional)

Room Setup

Make two paper signs, one marked with a large *X* and one marked with a large *O*. Tape these to the floor to mark where you want the contestants to stand.

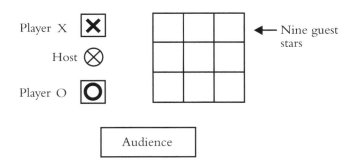

For the visual effect of a vertical square, arrange for the first three guest stars to sit on the floor, the next three to sit in chairs behind them, and the last three to stand behind the people in the chairs.

Preparing the Guest Stars

Recruit nine guest stars and give each one a name tag and a copy of the questions and answers for guest stars on pages 84–86. (Note: This set of questions and answers does not contain the tidbit statements found in the set for the host.) Meet with the guest stars privately. Let them know that every question the host will be asking is printed on the pages you gave them. With each question are a correct answer and an incorrect answer. They may respond with either one. Encourage them to be humorous with the contestants, even offering an initial response that is not listed on the resource. However, their final response must be one of the two choices on the pages.

Write a large *X* on each of nine sheets of paper. Turn the sheets over and write a large *O* on each one. Give one of these sheets to each guest star.

Game Directions

1. The host designates one contestant to control the *X*s and one to control the *O*s, directs them each to stand on the appropriate sign on the floor, and introduces them to the audience. The host then invites the guest stars to sit or stand in their designated spots, and introduces them.

2. The host flips a coin to determine which contestant goes first.

3. The first contestant selects a guest star. The host reads aloud for that star one of the questions from the set of questions and answers for the host on pages 77–83.

4. After the chosen guest star offers a final answer, the contestant decides whether the answer is true or false. The host reminds the audience not to help with that decision. The host announces whether the contestant is correct.

5. If the contestant is correct, the guest star holds up the mark that represents the contestant (either an *X* or an *O*) for the remainder of the game. If the contestant is not correct, the guest star holds up the opposing player's mark—unless doing so would result in a win. (Note: The opposing player cannot win the game because of an incorrect answer.)

6. After revealing the correct answer, the host takes a moment to add the corresponding tidbit statement. Everyone should keep in mind that the point of the game is for the young people to learn more about the church and their Catholic faith, not just to win.

7. After all the squares have been played, if neither player has three in a row, the winner is the player with the most marks being held up.

8. The host gives a prize to the winning player if prizes are being used.

Variations on the Game

Team play. After designating your guest stars, divide the remaining group into two teams to act as the two contestants. Select a captain to be the official spokesperson for each team.

Guest stars from outside the group. Recruit highly visible leaders in the parish or school—principals, pastors, parish council presidents, staff members, or other local personalities—to be the guest stars, and reserve the center square for the best known of those personalities. Or recruit young people from outside the group to serve as guest stars.

Numbered squares. If you do not have enough people to serve as guest stars, one option is to mark a ticktacktoe model on the floor or board and number the squares 1 through 9. Invite two contestants forward to play. Let the first contestant select a square, and then read aloud the question that corresponds to that square's number. Also read aloud one of the two responses. Instruct the contestant to answer true or false. If she or he is correct, award the square.

Invite the next contestant to select a new square from the remaining squares. Read aloud the corresponding question, and so on, until someone wins the game.

Free-for-all. If you do not have enough people to serve as guest stars, another option is to divide the group into two teams and invite the teams to be seated. Mark a ticktacktoe model on the floor or board, and number the squares 1 through 9. Read a question aloud, and let the teams try to answer it correctly. When someone thinks that they have the correct answer, they are to stand up and provide an answer immediately. If it is correct, they get to place their team's mark on any square they choose, by calling out the number of that square. If their answer is incorrect, the opposing team gets to guess the correct answer. If that team comes up with the correct answer, it gets a mark in the square. If it answers incorrectly, the square remains unmarked and another question is asked.

HOLY, HOLY, HOLY SQUARES—
QUESTIONS AND ANSWERS FOR THE HOST

1. What type of personal sin is considered the most serious?

Correct answer. mortal sin

Incorrect answer. original sin

Tidbit. There are two types of personal sin: venial and mortal. Venial sins are the "smaller, everyday" sins—such as lying, cheating, and gossiping—that turn us away from God and the community in some way. Sins of this kind hurt our relationships with God and with one another. Mortal sins are considered by the church to be extremely serious because they result from deliberate decisions to do evil, such as murder and abortion, and therefore they cut us off from God. The sacrament of Reconciliation is used to bring us back into a right relationship with God through the admission of our sins to a priest.

2. The first reading heard at Sunday Mass is usually taken from which part of the Scriptures?

Correct answer. the Old Testament

Incorrect answer. the New Testament

Tidbit. The first reading is usually taken from the Old Testament, as is the psalm response sung after the first reading. The second reading is taken from the New Testament, and the Gospel reading is taken from one of the four Gospels (Matthew, Mark, Luke, and John). The book from which the lectors proclaim these readings at Mass is called the lectionary.

3. Who is the third person of the Trinity?

Correct answer. the Holy Spirit

Incorrect answer. the Son (Jesus)

Tidbit. The Trinity is a foundational doctrine of Catholics that reveals God as one person expressed in three different ways—God as Father, God as Son, and God as the Holy Spirit. While each of these expressions takes a different form, they all still remain one being—God.

4. The teaching that Jesus is both human and divine was affirmed at which ecumenical council?

Correct answer. the Council of Chalcedon

Incorrect answer. the Council of Trent

Tidbit. The Council of Chalcedon was the fourth major ecumenical council, or gathering of bishops, held so that the church could discern core teachings of the Catholic faith. In October 451, Emperor Marcian, Empress Pulcheria, and Pope Leo I called together over six hundred bishops to help develop the belief that Jesus Christ has two natures—human and divine.

5. The official teachings of the church are known as what?

Correct answer. doctrines

Incorrect answer. canon law

Tidbit. Doctrines are the official teachings of the church and are developed by an ecumenical council, a pope, or a gathering of bishops in union with the pope. Dogmas are specific doctrines that are essential to the faith and cannot be changed.

6. Who elects a pope?

Correct answer. the College of Cardinals

Incorrect answer. the College of Bishops

Tidbit. Only bishops who have been selected as cardinals gather together to choose a pope from among themselves. The gathering of cardinals, called the College of Cardinals, numbers no more than 120 and stays behind locked doors in the Vatican until a pope is selected. When the cardinals have reached a decision, they send up white smoke through the chimney to signal to the world that a new pope has been elected.

7. Who takes vows of poverty, chastity, and obedience?

Correct answer. religious sisters and brothers

Incorrect answer. diocesan priests

Tidbit. Diocesan priests' vows do not include poverty, although their Christian faith invites them to lead a life of justice and service.

Religious sisters and brothers are members of religious orders, with each community known for its own particular mission, service, or geographic area.

8. What is an outward sign instituted by Christ to give grace?

Correct answer. a sacrament

Incorrect answer. a revelation

Tidbit. The Catholic church celebrates seven sacraments: Anointing of the Sick, Baptism, Confirmation, the Eucharist, Holy Orders, Matrimony, and Reconciliation. Each sacrament has specific symbols and rituals associated with it. Each sacrament allows the faithful to fully celebrate and participate in the deep meaning and grace it offers.

9. How many theses made up Martin Luther's call for reform in 1517?

Correct answer. ninety-five

Incorrect answer. seventy-five

Tidbit. Martin Luther was an Augustinian priest who lived in a monastery in Wittenberg, Germany. He sent to the archbishop of a neighboring town, Mainz, a letter that contained his now famous Ninety-five Theses. The theses outlined concerns about abuses of the church, including the selling of indulgences and the reliance on external practices and prayers to "earn" God's grace. Luther's Ninety-five Theses became the touchstone for the Protestant Reformation.

10. Pope John XXIII convened which ecumenical council?

Correct answer. Vatican Council II

Incorrect answer. the Council of Trent

Tidbit. Pope John XXIII called for an ecumenical council in 1959 and convened Vatican Council II in 1962. He died a year later and so was not alive to see its conclusion in 1965 and its impact on the way people of this generation experience church and celebrate Mass.

11. Which sacrament was once called Extreme Unction?

Correct answer. Anointing of the Sick

Incorrect answer. Holy Orders

Tidbit. Extreme Unction and *Last Rights* are names once ascribed to the sacrament of the Anointing of the Sick. The new name helps place the sacrament in the proper context because the sacrament is meant for all who feel ill, physically or mentally, and not just for those on their deathbed.

12. Who makes an *Ad Limina* visit?

Correct answer. bishops

Incorrect answer. pastors

Tidbit. Each bishop is required to make a pilgrimage to Rome every three to ten years. During this visit, called an *Ad Limina Apostolorum* (meaning "to the threshold of the Apostles"), the bishop tells the pope what is happening within his diocese.

13. How many lectionary cycles are there?

Correct answer. three

Incorrect answer. five

Tidbit. The church has developed three lectionary cycles, each one focusing on a particular Gospel and a related set of Old and New Testament readings. These are the readings we hear proclaimed at Mass. Cycle A focuses primarily on the Gospel of Matthew, Cycle B focuses on Mark and some of John, and Cycle C focuses on Luke. Each year, a new cycle begins the first week of Advent and concludes on Christ the King Sunday. Therefore, in the course of three years, people attending church hear a major portion of the New Testament and most of the key readings from the Old Testament.

14. What does the Assumption celebrate?

Correct answer. Mary's body's assumption into heaven after her death

Incorrect answer. Jesus' return to heaven after Pentecost

Tidbit. The feast of the Assumption, a holy day of obligation for Catholics, is celebrated on 15 August to honor the person of Mary and the belief that, upon her death, she was assumed—body and soul—into heaven.

15. What prayer is prayed the most when using the rosary?

Correct answer. the Hail Mary

Incorrect answer. the Lord's Prayer

Tidbit. The rosary is a prayer form that helps people focus on the life of Mary and the central role she played in God's revelation. The Hail Mary is prayed fifty times during the recitation of the rosary.

16. What does *RCIA* stand for?

Correct answer. Rite of Christian Initiation of Adults

Incorrect answer. Roman Catholic Initiation of Adults

Tidbit. The RCIA is the process adults enter to become full members of the Catholic church. It is open to any adult who has not been fully initiated (who has not received one or more of the sacraments of Baptism, the Eucharist, and Confirmation). Adults who go through the RCIA enter the church, or complete their initiation, during the Easter Vigil on Holy Saturday.

17. Which liturgical season is marked by a spirit of penitence?

Correct answer. Lent

Incorrect answer. Advent

Tidbit. The forty days of Lent begin on Ash Wednesday and end on Holy Thursday. They are marked by penitence, prayer, fasting, and abstinence from meat on Fridays, as a way of spiritually preparing for the celebration of Easter.

18. Giving away a portion of one's income, usually one-tenth, is referred to as what?

Correct answer. tithing

Incorrect answer. making an offertory

Tidbit. Tithing dates back to Old Testament times and can refer to giving away a portion of money or land. It is a way for those who "have" to share with those who "have not." Many churches invite their members to tithe for their place of worship and for agencies that support people in need.

19. What month is traditionally set aside for honoring Mary?

Correct answer. May

Incorrect answer. August

Tidbit. May is the month that has traditionally focused on the Blessed Mother. During this month, statues of Mary are crowned, often on the thirty-first (formerly a celebration of the queenship of Mary, now the feast of the Visitation).

20. What was the original meaning of the word *catholic?*

Correct answer. "universal"

Incorrect answer. "holy"

Tidbit. The term *catholic* has its origins in ancient times, after the entire Roman Empire had converted to Christianity, making Christianity a catholic, or universal, church. The Catholic church is not only universal but also multicultural, with a universal vision and perspective that identify every person as a unique creation of God and each individual as called to holiness.

21. Who is sometimes referred to as the Vicar of Christ?

Correct answer. the pope

Incorrect answer. Saint Paul

Tidbit. The pope is referred to as the Vicar of Christ. The papal office originated with Saint Peter and has been passed on, through succession, to each pope, with all popes serving as the bishop of Rome but with universal authority over the church.

22. What do we call the offices and people through whom the pope administers the church?

Correct answer. the Roman curia

Incorrect answer. the Vatican Council

Tidbit. The Roman curia is the collection of people and offices that help the pope run the church. It is similar to the cabinet of the U.S. president in that its leaders advise the pope on matters of importance to the church. The pope's "right-hand man" is known as the cardinal secretary of state, and acts as a gatekeeper to all information and issues that are brought before the pope.

23. What are the three types of mysteries recited in the rosary?

Correct answer. the joyful, sorrowful, and glorious mysteries

Incorrect answer. the divine, paschal, and holy mysteries

Tidbit. The three types of mysteries that are recited in the rosary refer to events in the life of Jesus Christ. The joyful mysteries focus on the Incarnation (birth of Jesus), the sorrowful mysteries focus on Jesus' Passion and death, and the glorious mysteries focus on Jesus' Resurrection. Each time someone prays the rosary, they select at least one of the types of mysteries to focus on. Each type includes five events from the life of Jesus, and each event is reflected on as each decade of the rosary is prayed.

24. Sacred actions and objects are referred to as what?

Correct answer. sacramentals

Incorrect answer. blessed

Tidbit. Sacramentals are the sacred objects, actions, and gestures that the church uses in either public or private devotions. They include holy water, incense, the sign of the cross, blessed palms, holy oils, rosaries, and sprinkling with water.

25. Who is considered the father of Western monasticism because of his Rule?

Correct answer. Saint Benedict

Incorrect answer. Pope Gregory the Great

Tidbit. Benedict built a monastery at the top of a mountain between Rome and Naples in 529 and called it Monte Cassino. There he developed what has become known as the Rule of Benedict, which eventually became the basic guide for living in religious communities in the West. The various points of the Rule stress a balance between work and prayer.

HOLY, HOLY, HOLY SQUARES—
QUESTIONS AND ANSWERS FOR GUEST STARS

1. What type of personal sin is considered the most serious?
Correct answer. mortal sin
Incorrect answer. original sin

2. The first reading heard at Sunday Mass is usually taken from which part of the Scriptures?
Correct answer. the Old Testament
Incorrect answer. the New Testament

3. Who is the third person of the Trinity?
Correct answer. the Holy Spirit
Incorrect answer. the Son (Jesus)

4. The teaching that Jesus is both human and divine was affirmed at which ecumenical council?
Correct answer. the Council of Chalcedon
Incorrect answer. the Council of Trent

5. The official teachings of the church are known as what?
Correct answer. doctrines
Incorrect answer. canon law

6. Who elects a pope?
Correct answer. the College of Cardinals
Incorrect answer. the College of Bishops

7. Who takes vows of poverty, chastity, and obedience?
Correct answer. religious sisters and brothers
Incorrect answer. diocesan priests

8. What is an outward sign instituted by Christ to give grace?
Correct answer. a sacrament
Incorrect answer. a revelation

9. How many theses made up Martin Luther's call for reform in 1517?
Correct answer. ninety-five
Incorrect answer. seventy-five

10. Pope John XXIII convened which ecumenical council?
Correct answer. Vatican Council II
Incorrect answer. the Council of Trent

11. Which sacrament was once called Extreme Unction?
Correct answer. Anointing of the Sick
Incorrect answer. Holy Orders

12. Who makes an *Ad Limina* visit?
Correct answer. bishops
Incorrect answer. pastors

13. How many lectionary cycles are there?
Correct answer. three
Incorrect answer. five

14. What does the Assumption celebrate?
Correct answer. Mary's body's assumption into heaven after her death
Incorrect answer. Jesus' return to heaven after Pentecost

15. What prayer is prayed the most when using the rosary?
Correct answer. the Hail Mary
Incorrect answer. the Lord's Prayer

16. What does *RCIA* stand for?
Correct answer. Rite of Christian Initiation of Adults
Incorrect answer. Roman Catholic Initiation of Adults

17. Which liturgical season is marked by a spirit of penitence?
Correct answer. Lent
Incorrect answer. Advent

18. Giving away a portion of one's income, usually one-tenth, is referred to as what?

Correct answer. tithing
Incorrect answer. making an offertory

19. What month is traditionally set aside for honoring Mary?
Correct answer. May
Incorrect answer. August

20. What was the original meaning of the word *catholic?*
Correct answer. "universal"
Incorrect answer. "holy"

21. Who is sometimes referred to as the Vicar of Christ?
Correct answer. the pope
Incorrect answer. Saint Paul

22. What do we call the offices and people through whom the pope administers the church?

Correct answer. the Roman curia
Incorrect answer. the Vatican Council

23. What are the three types of mysteries recited in the rosary?
Correct answer. the joyful, sorrowful, and glorious mysteries
Incorrect answer. the divine, paschal, and holy mysteries

24. Sacred actions and objects are referred to as what?
Correct answer. sacramentals
Incorrect answer. blessed

25. Who is considered the father of Western monasticism because of his Rule?

Correct answer. Saint Benedict
Incorrect answer. Pope Gregory the Great

Permission to reproduce this page for program use is granted.

THE CHURCH IS RIGHT

Object of the Game

Modeled after the game show *The Price Is Right,* this game begins with four audience members being invited to "come on down" and be contestants. The contestants are asked to answer a numerical question about church history or the Catholic faith. The contestant whose response is closest to the actual answer without going over it is invited to compete individually in a second round, which tests his or her knowledge of Catholic facts and faith. Ten questions and answers are provided for each round.

HOW THE GAME IS PLAYED

Players

- ☐ one host
- ☐ four contestants for each set of rounds (called from the audience)
- ☐ one scorekeeper
- ☐ one timekeeper

Supplies

- ☐ newsprint and markers
- ☐ pencils and slips of paper
- ☐ a basket
- ☐ a watch or clock that displays seconds
- ☐ prizes (optional)

Room Setup

Contestants

Prize table (optional)

Round 2 table

Scorekeeper

Host

Audience

Round Two Setup

Copy the lists for second-round questions 1, 4, and 5, from pages 95–97, onto separate sheets of newsprint or overhead transparencies. Be sure that you do not copy the answers. Photocopy pages 101–104 for second-round questions 2, 3, 8, and 9; cut apart the lists as scored; and clip each list in order. You might want to attach a self-stick note to each list, indicating the number of the question it is for. Keep the lists out of sight near the round 2 table until the questions are asked. When it is time for each question, post the corresponding list so that all can see, or give the contestant the clipped stack of list items. Provide writing materials (such as newsprint and a marker, a chalkboard and chalk, or a white board and a marker) for questions that call for a written response, and tape or tacks for posting the cut-apart items in order.

Near the round 2 table, provide a blank sheet of newsprint and a marker, a chalkboard and chalk, or a white board and a marker, for recording the round 2 contestants' names and point totals.

Game Directions

Round One

1. The host invites the participants to write their name on a slip of paper and place it in a basket. The host reads the introductory script from page 91, or uses her or his own words to introduce the game. Then the host picks the names of four people from the basket and invites each of those people to "come on down."

2. After the contestants introduce themselves, the host begins with a round 1 question from pages 92–94. She or he invites the players to answer the question, beginning with the *last* player called from the audience and proceeding in order to the first person called. No two contestants may offer the same answer.

3. The player whose response is closest to the correct number without going over it moves on to round 2. If all guesses are higher than the correct answer, the contestants try again until someone comes closest without going over.

4. The host might want to provide the winner of round 1 with a small prize such as a bite-size candy bar or a bookmark.

Round Two

1. The winner of round 1 is invited "onstage" (to the round 2 table) and given a round 2 question from pages 95–104 to solve. The round 2 questions are all timed, so someone must keep track of the

elapsed time. Each answer has seven parts, and the contestant receives 7 points for each part that is answered correctly, so each question is worth a possible total of 49 points. The scorekeeper adds up the contestant's points and writes them next to the player's name on a posted sheet of newsprint.

2. After the contestant has completed round 2, she or he rejoins the audience.

3. The host picks another name out of the basket and invites that person to "come on down" to join the other three contestants waiting to win a chance to go to round 2. This person will be the first to respond to the next round 1 question. Once again, the contestant whose answer is closest to the correct answer without going over it plays round 2.

4. The group continues this cycle until it runs out of time or questions. The grand winner is the contestant who gets the most points during her or his turn at round 2. The host gives this person a "grand prize" if prizes are being used. In a tie, the grand prize can be shared.

Prizes

If you decide to use prizes, try to secure donations from area businesses frequented by young people (such as fast-food restaurants, record stores, amusement parks, bowling alleys, and dollar stores). Also consider offering prizes the young people can use in their classroom or school (no-homework passes, free-lunch passes, and so on). Separate the donations into grand prizes, round 2 prizes, and round 1 prizes. Display them so that all the contestants know what they are competing for.

Variations on the Game

Assistants. Recruit two assistants to bring out the round 2 questions, deliver prizes, and call out the name of the next contestant to "come on down." Give them each a saint's name, such as Saint Joan of Arc, Saint Thérèse of Lisieux, Saint Thomas More, or Saint Augustine. Perhaps even encourage the assistants to dress up as their character.

Team play. To involve the entire group, divide everyone into four or more teams. Label every team with a letter (team A, team B, and so on), and ask each team to select a spokesperson to give its responses after the team members have discussed the questions. Conduct rounds 1 and 2 as described in the game directions, treating each team as a single contestant.

INTRODUCTORY SCRIPT

To add some humor and lightheartedness to the game, consider having the host begin with the following script or an adaptation of it:

> Good afternoon, and welcome to another edition of "The Church Is Right"! I'm the star and host of the show, Bob Talker. As you know, this is the show that invites four lucky people from our studio audience (that's you) to "come on down" and try your luck at some questions about Catholic facts and faith.
>
> There are two rounds to each part of the game. The first round is based on numbers associated with church history and Catholic facts, and will determine the lucky contestant who will be able to stand next to me, your host and star, Bob Talker! Not only that, but that special someone will also get the opportunity to answer a round 2 question based on Catholic beliefs and events. Each round 2 contestant can score up to 49 points. The round 2 contestant with the highest score by the end of the show will be declared our grand-prize winner, which means that she or he will get a second chance to stand here next to me, your star and host, Bob Talker! As if that were not enough, the grand-prize winner will also be able to take home a grand prize.
>
> And now, let's see who our first four contestants will be. [The host pulls four names out of the basket, one at a time, announcing each name followed by the words: "Come on down! You are the next contestant on 'The Church Is Right'!"]

THE CHURCH IS RIGHT—QUESTIONS AND ANSWERS

Round One

1. How many popes served in the twentieth century?

Answer. nine

Tidbit. The nine twentieth-century popes were as follows: Leo XIII (1878–1903), Pius X (1903–1914), Benedict XV (1914–1922), Pius XI (1922–1939), Pius XII (1939–1958), John XXIII (1958–1963), Paul VI (1963–1978), John Paul I (1978), and John Paul II (1978–).

2. What year did the Council of Trent begin?

Answer. 1545

Tidbit. The Council of Trent began on 13 December 1545 with thirty bishops in attendance, and continued to meet off and on over the next eighteen years. The council marked the beginning of the Counter-Reformation and defined key doctrinal issues such as the importance of the Scriptures and Tradition, the seven sacraments, transubstantiation, and the hierarchical church.

3. What year did Christianity become a universal religion?

Answer. 313

Tidbit. In 312, before a key battle with Maxentius, the chosen Roman emperor Constantine had a vision of Christ. After winning the battle, Constantine converted to Christianity and ruled the Western part of the Roman Empire. In 313, he and the Eastern emperor issued the Edict of Milan, which made it the favored religion of the Roman Empire. For the first time, Christians were able to celebrate their faith without the threat of persecution.

4. When did the Protestant Reformation start?

Answer. 1517

Tidbit. The Reformation as we know it was a sixteenth-century movement aimed at church reform. The movement originated from Martin Luther's Ninety-five Theses, which cited controversy over indulgences (remissions for sins) granted by the church. The movement eventually led to the emergence of several Protestant churches, though its intent was at first reform, not separation.

5. When was Saint Peter's Basilica completed?

Answer. 1626

Tidbit. Saint Peter's Basilica is located in the Vatican City and is the home church of the pope. It is also one of the largest churches in the world, covering about 4 acres. Its bell, rung on special occasions, weighs 10 tons.

6. When was Francis of Assisi born?

Answer. 1182

Tidbit. Saint Francis of Assisi was the rich son of a clothing merchant who had a profound conversion experience after which he literally stripped himself of all material possessions and began preaching and serving the poor, ill, and scorned members of his society. Many people began following Francis, and they became the first members of the Franciscan order.

7. When did Vatican Council I begin?

Answer. 1869

Tidbit. Vatican Council I is perhaps most widely known for its declaration of papal infallibility. The council also initiated an intense and vibrant spiritual rebirth of Catholicism and its traditions, resulting in the Catholic church's becoming a worldwide influence as it entered the twentieth century.

8. How many books are in a Catholic Bible?

Answer. seventy-three

Tidbit. Catholic Bibles have seven more books than do most Protestant Bibles. Those extra books are often referred to as the apocryphal, or deuterocanonical, books.

9. According to the *Catechism of the Catholic Church*, how many precepts of the church are there?

Answer. five

Tidbit. The five precepts, or duties, of all Catholic Christians, as outlined by the Catholic church, are these:

- To attend Mass on Sundays and holy days of obligation and to rest from servile labor
- To confess one's (serious) sins at least once a year
- To receive the sacrament of the Eucharist at least during the Easter season
- To observe days of fasting and abstinence established by the church
- To provide for the needs of the church

10. What is the number, signified by Roman numerals, following the name of the pope who began Vatican Council II?

Answer. twenty-three

Tidbit. Pope John XXIII began the Second Vatican Council on 11 October 1962. This council was responsible for bringing the church into the modern world and resulted in many changes, most notably the use of native languages rather than Latin for celebrating the Mass, increased roles for laypeople at Mass, and the priest's turning around so that he faced the people during the liturgy of the Eucharist.

Round Two

1. Complete these sentences from traditional Catholic prayers and creeds. If you are stumped, you may yell "Pass" to move on to the next sentence, and if you have time at the end, you may return to any sentences you have not completed. You have 60 seconds beginning now! [Note to host: Read one phrase at a time and allow the contestant a chance to answer.]

List
1. Holy Mary, mother of God . . .
2. Through him, with him, in him . . .
3. Glory to the Father . . .
4. We believe in one Lord, Jesus Christ . . .
5. Give us this day our daily bread . . .
6. I confess to almighty God . . .
7. For you alone are the Holy One . . .

Answer
1. pray for us sinners,
   now and at the hour of our death.

   [From the Hail Mary]
2. in the unity of the Holy Spirit, all glory and honor is yours,
   almighty Father, for ever and ever. [From the Final Doxology]
3. and to the Son,
   and to the Holy Spirit:
   As it was in the beginning, is now,
   and will be for ever.

   [From the Glory Be, or Glory to the Father]
4. the only Son of God
   eternally begotten of the Father,
   God from God, Light from Light,
   true God from true God,
   begotten, not made, one in Being with the Father.

   [From the Nicene Creed]

5. and forgive us our trespasses,
     as we forgive those who trespass against us,
     and lead us not into temptation,
     but deliver us from evil.

[From the Lord's Prayer]

6. and to you, my brothers and sisters,
     that I have sinned through my own fault
     in my thoughts and in my words,
     in what I have done,
     and in what I have failed to do.

[From the Confiteor]

7. you alone are the Lord,
     you alone are the Most High,
          Jesus Christ,
          with the Holy Spirit,
          in the glory of God the Father.

[From the Gloria, or Glory to God in the Highest]

2. You have 60 seconds to place these parts of the Mass in the order in which they occur. [Note to host: Give the contestant the list items you copied from page 101.]

Answer
1. penitential rite
2. responsorial psalm
3. profession of faith
4. eucharistic prayer
5. Lord's Prayer
6. Lamb of God
7. dismissal

3. You have 60 seconds to place these holy days and feasts in the order in which they occur during the liturgical year. [Note to host: Give the contestant the list items you copied from page 102.]

Answer

1. Christmas Day (25 December)
2. the solemnity of Mary, Mother of God (1 January)
3. Ash Wednesday (the beginning of Lent)
4. Easter (the holiest day of the liturgical year)
5. Pentecost (approximately fifty days after Easter)
6. All Saints' Day (1 November)
7. Christ the King Sunday (always the last Sunday of the liturgical year)

4. For each of these events, state whether it is a joyful, sorrowful, or glorious mystery (used in praying the rosary). You have 60 seconds beginning now. [Note to host: Read one event at a time and allow the contestant a chance to answer.]

List	*Answer*
the Visitation	joyful
the Ascension	glorious
the finding of Jesus in the Temple	joyful
the carrying of the cross	sorrowful
the Resurrection	glorious
the Crucifixion	sorrowful
the Annunciation	joyful

5. Unscramble each of these words to come up with the seven capital, or "deadly," sins. You have 60 seconds beginning now.

List	*Answer*
epidr	pride
noscveotuses	covetousness
stul	lust
eagnr	anger
ntlygout·	gluttony
yevn	envy
hoslt	sloth

6. In 60 seconds, verbally list the seven gifts of the Holy Spirit.

Answer
wisdom
understanding
counsel (or right judgment)
fortitude (or courage)
knowledge
piety (or reverence)
fear of the Lord (or wonder and awe)

7. In 60 seconds, verbally list the seven sacraments of the Catholic church, beginning with the sacraments of initiation.

Answer
Baptism
the Eucharist
Confirmation
Reconciliation
Anointing of the Sick
Matrimony
Holy Orders

8. You have 60 seconds to place these events in the order in which they appear in the traditional stations of the cross. [Note to host: Give the contestant the list items you copied from page 103.]

Answer
1. Jesus is condemned to death.
2. Jesus meets his mother.
3. Simon of Cyrene helps Jesus carry his cross.
4. Jesus falls a third time.
5. Jesus is nailed to the cross.
6. Jesus dies on the cross.
7. Jesus is placed in the tomb.

9. Place these events of church history in the order in which they occurred, beginning with the earliest. You have 60 seconds beginning now. [Note to host: Give the contestant the list items you copied from page 104.]

Answer

1. Pentecost (the "birthday" of the church)
2. the Edict of Milan, making Christianity a universal religion (pronounced in 313 by Emperor Constantine and the Eastern Roman emperor)
3. the first Council of Nicaea (began in 325 and developed the original Nicene Creed)
4. Saint Benedict's establishment of monasteries throughout Europe (began in 520 as Benedict started to convert many of the barbarians who had invaded Europe after the fall of Rome)
5. the Protestant Reformation (began in 1517 when Martin Luther sent his Ninety-five Theses to the church of Wittenberg)
6. the Council of Trent and the Counter-Reformation (began in 1545 as a response to the Protestant Reformation, and solidified certain key Catholic doctrines)
7. Vatican Council II (began in 1962 and directed many changes in the liturgy that resulted in the church's entering the modern era)

10. Respond yes or no to indicate whether the Catholic church in the United States considers these celebrations to be holy days of obligation. You have 60 seconds to respond verbally, beginning now.

List	*Answer*
Ash Wednesday	no
the Immaculate Conception (8 December)	yes
the solemnity of Mary, Mother of God (1 January)	yes
the Annunciation (25 March)	no
Holy Thursday	no
the Assumption (15 August)	yes
All Souls' Day (2 November)	no

[Note to host: The other holy days of obligation observed in the United States are Christmas (25 December), the Ascension (the sixth Thursday after Easter), and All Saints' Day (1 November).]

Lord's Prayer

responsorial psalm

eucharistic prayer

LAMB OF GOD

dismissal

profession of faith

PENITENTIAL RITE

PENTECOST

Ash Wednesday

Christ the King Sunday

Christmas Day

All Saints' Day

EASTER

the solemnity of
Mary, Mother of God

Jesus is placed in the tomb.

Jesus falls a third time.

JESUS MEETS HIS MOTHER.

Jesus is nailed to the cross.

Jesus is condemned to death.

Simon of Cyrene helps Jesus carry his cross.

Jesus dies on the cross.

the Protestant Reformation

the visitation of the Holy Spirit that is now celebrated at Pentecost

Saint Benedict's establishment of monasteries throughout Europe

VATICAN COUNCIL II

the Council of Trent and the Counter-Reformation

the Edict of Milan, making Christianity a universal religion

THE FIRST COUNCIL OF NICAEA

THE REAL FORTUNE

Object of the Game

Like contestants in the popular game show *Wheel of Fortune,* contestants in this game attempt to solve word puzzles by guessing or purchasing letters in the phrases after they spin a wheel (or roll a die) to see how many points they will get for each letter they guess correctly. In this version of the game, all the puzzles are related to Catholic beliefs and practices.

HOW THE GAME IS PLAYED

Players

- [ ] one host
- [ ] three contestants (chosen from the audience)
- [ ] one scorekeeper

Supplies

- [ ] a spinner created from a copy of the diagram on page 111 (or a die)
- [ ] a copy of the phrases on pages 112–119, for the scorekeeper
- [ ] a score sheet for each phrase (see the score sheet setup instructions on page 107)
- [ ] prizes (optional)

Room Setup

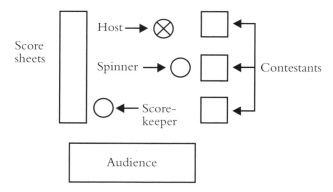

Spinner Setup

Copy the wheel from page 111 onto heavy paper and cut it out. Cut a pointer from the same paper. Cut or punch a ⅛-inch hole in the bottom of the pointer and in the center of the wheel. Push a round-head paper fastener through the hole in the pointer and then through the center of the wheel, and open the fastener so that it is secure but allows the pointer to spin freely.

If you prefer, omit the spinner and instead provide a die to be rolled, with the number of dots on the sides of the die corresponding to the numbered wedges on the wheel. You may want to post a copy of the spinner for reference.

Score Sheet Setup

This game uses the phrases on pages 112–119, which are divided into four categories—"Sacraments," "Historical Happenings," "Church Life," and "Who's Who." Before the game, decide which phrases you will use, and plan to alternate categories throughout the game.

Use the following model to create a score sheet for each phrase that you select. Be sure to draw one underline for each letter in the phrase, leave extra spaces between the words, and fill in any punctuation marks. The score sheets can be created on newsprint, poster board, overhead transparencies, a chalkboard, PowerPoint displays, or whatever works best for you.

Category: _____

Score: Incorrect
Player 1: _____   letters guessed:
Player 2: _____
Player 3: _____

Phrase to be solved

— — —   — — —   — — —   — — —

Game Directions

1. The host selects three contestants from the audience and introduces them and the scorekeeper to the audience. The host explains the rules of the game and how the score will be kept.

2. Each contestant spins the spinner (or rolls the die). The contestant with the highest number goes first. The host introduces the phrase to be guessed, by calling out its category ("Sacraments," "Historical Happenings," "Church Life," or "Who's Who").

3. The first contestant spins the spinner. The contestant then names a consonant she or he thinks is in the phrase. If the letter is in the phrase, the scorekeeper writes it in each underlined blank that it appears. The contestant is then awarded a score for that turn, equal to the amount on the spinner multiplied by the number of times the letter is in the phrase. Say the contestant's spin lands on "3 Blessings" and the contestant then guesses the letter N. If N appears two times in the phrase, the contestant gets 6 blessings added to her or his score.

4. If a contestant correctly guesses a letter that appears in the phrase, she or he gets to spin and guess again. If a contestant guesses a letter that is not in the phrase, her or his turn ends and the next contestant gets a turn.

5. If a contestant's spin lands on "Lose a turn," the contestant loses her or his turn, and the next contestant gets a turn.

6. A contestant wins by naming the phrase exactly. A contestant may try to guess the phrase at any point during her or his turn. The contestant must first say, "I'd like to solve the phrase," and then state her or his guess. The host announces whether the guess is correct. If it is correct, the contestant is declared the winner. If it is incorrect, the contestant must sit out until the puzzle is solved correctly by another contestant.

7. Vowels (A, E, I, O, and U) cannot be guessed; they must be purchased for 3 blessings each. A contestant may buy a vowel only during her or his turn—either before or after a spin. The contestant says, "I'd like to buy a vowel," and names the vowel. If the vowel is in

the phrase, the scorekeeper writes all the occurrences in the correct blanks. Three blessings are subtracted from the contestant's score, no matter how many times the vowel appears. The contestant may then either attempt to guess the phrase or spin the spinner.

8. If all the consonants in a phrase are guessed and only vowels remain, the host indicates that and gives the contestant at the spinner an opportunity to buy a vowel or solve the puzzle. If the contestant is incorrect, the next contestant takes a turn.

9. Once a phrase is solved, prizes are awarded if they are being used. Then the two contestants who did not solve it return to the audience, and the winner is joined by two new contestants for a new game with another phrase.

Host Instructions

The host is responsible for beginning the game, choosing and introducing the contestants, controlling the flow of the game, declaring the winner, and awarding prizes if they are used.

After a puzzle is solved, the host invites everyone to share what they know about the particular person, sacrament, object, or occurrence that is named in the answer. The host offers the tidbit information provided with the phrase, and any other insights she or he has about the answer.

Scorekeeper Instructions

Referring to a copy of the phrases on pages 112–119, the scorekeeper determines if a contestant guesses a correct letter, writes each correct letter in the appropriate underlined blank or blanks, and then calculates the blessings earned and adds them to the contestant's score on the score sheet. If a contestant guesses an incorrect letter, the scorekeeper writes it on the right-hand side of the score sheet. When a puzzle is solved, the scorekeeper writes in the full answer on the score sheet.

Prizes

If you choose to use prizes, award the winners of each puzzle a medium or large prize, and the other two contestants a small prize. Or invite the winners each to purchase a prize using the blessings they collect. For example, they might buy a small prize for between 1 and 10 blessings, a medium prize for between 11 and 20 blessings, or a large prize for over 20 blessings. Winners could save their blessings to add to what they might win in the future, in order to purchase a larger prize.

Variations on the Game

Team or family play. Divide the group into three teams of two or three people, or have three families (or parent-child teams) play. From each team, select a captain to be its official spokesperson.

Group play. Give everyone in the group a turn spinning the spinner (or rolling the die) and choosing a letter, one person at a time. After a phrase is solved, continue with a new phrase.

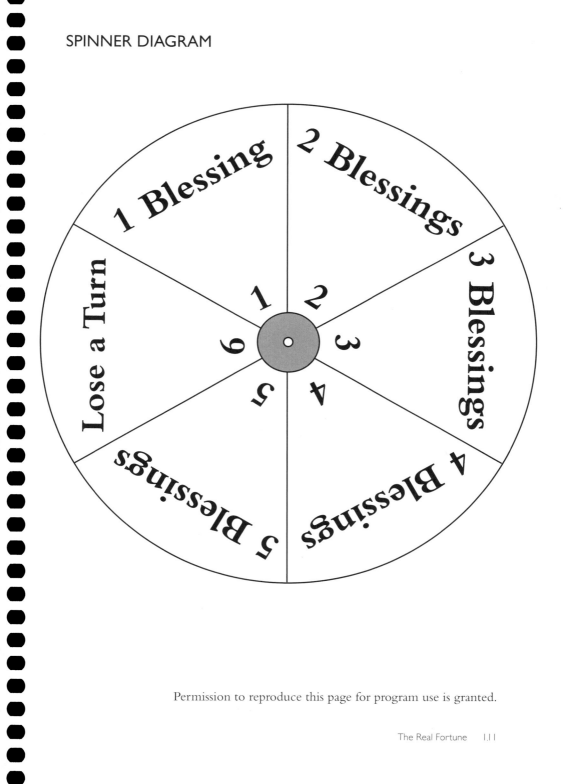

THE REAL FORTUNE—PHRASES

The phrases used for the answers in this game are divided into the following four categories, and the categories should be alternated in their use:

- "Sacraments"
- "Historical Happenings"
- "Church Life"
- "Who's Who"

After each answer, the letters used in the phrase are listed. If a letter is used more than once, the number of times it is used is included in parentheses.

Category: Sacraments

1. *Answer.* B A P T I S M, T H E E U C H A R I S T, A N D C O N F I R M A T I O N

Letters used. A (4), B (1), C (2), D (1), E (2), F (1), H (2), I (4), M (2), N (3), O (2), P (1), R (2), S (2), T (4), U (1)

Tidbit. These three sacraments together are referred to as the sacraments of initiation. Upon reception of all three, an individual is considered fully initiated into the Catholic church.

2. *Answer.* L A Y I N G O N O F H A N D S

Letters used. A (2), D (1), F (1), G (1), H (1), I (1), L (1), N (3), O (2), S (1), Y (1)

Tidbit. This prayerful gesture occurs when a priest or bishop lays his hands on the head of an individual. It is found in the sacraments of Anointing of the Sick, Confirmation, and Holy Orders. It can be used in other situations, such as during a commissioning or healing service as the presider prays silently or aloud.

3. *Answer.* E X A M I N A T I O N O F C O N S C I E N C E

Permission to reproduce this page for program use is granted.

Letters used. A (2), C (3), E (3), F (1), I (3), M (1), N (4), O (3), S (1), T (1), X (1)

Tidbit. An examination of conscience is performed in the Reconciliation rite before an individual goes to confession. The assembled are invited to reflect on the ways they have turned away from God through sin, so that each can enter confession fully prepared to admit her or his faults and turn them over to God in order to experience God's mercy and forgiveness.

4. *Answer.* T H E   L I T U R G Y   O F   T H E   E U C H A R I S T

Letters used. A (1), C (1), E (3), F (1), G (1), H (3), I (2), L (1), O (1), R (2), S (1), T (4), U (2), Y (1)

Tidbit. The liturgy of the Eucharist is the third part of the Mass (following the introductory rite and the liturgy of the word). During the liturgy of the Eucharist, the gifts are prepared, brought to the altar, and prayed over. The eucharistic prayer is prayed by the celebrant, and the Communion rite occurs. The last part of the Mass, the concluding rite, follows the liturgy of the Eucharist.

5. *Answer.* T H E   M A R R I A G E   V O W S

Letters used. A (2), E (2), G (1), H (1), I (1), M (1), O (1), R (2), S (1), T (1), V (1), W (1)

Tidbit. The marriage vows are offered between the bride and groom during the wedding rite of the sacrament of Matrimony. The vows are the couple's public promises to love, honor, and commit to each other for the rest of their lives. After the vows are spoken aloud, the couple bless and exchange wedding rings as a visible sign of their promises.

Category: Historical Happenings

1. *Answer.* T H E   C O N V E R S I O N   O F   C O N S T A N T I N E

Letters used. A (1), C (2), E (3), F (1), H (1), I (2), N (5), O (4), R (1), S (2), T (3),V (1)

Tidbit. Constantine, the chosen ruler of the Roman Empire, had a vision in A.D. 312, before a major battle. As a result of that vision, he instructed his soldiers to paint the Greek letters *XP (Chi-Rho)*, the first two letters in the name of Christ, on their banners and shields. His army won, and Constantine began to rule the Western part of the empire. In 313, along with the ruler of the Eastern part of the empire, he implemented the Edict of Milan, which allowed Christians to worship freely throughout the Roman Empire for the first time in history.

2. *Answer.* T H E   P R O T E S T A N T   R E F O R M A T I O N

Letters used. A (2), E (3), F (1), H (1), I (1), M (1), N (2), O (3), P (1), R (3), S (1),T (5)

Tidbit. In 1517, Martin Luther, an Augustinian priest who lived at the monastery in Wittenberg, Germany, sent Prince-Archbishop Albert of Mainz a letter outlining the abuses he saw in the church at the time. The now famous letter, known as the Ninety-five Thesis, touched off the Protestant Reformation, which among other things called for a stop to the selling of indulgences and to relying on external practices to achieve salvation.

3. *Answer.* T H E   S E C O N D   V A T I C A N   C O U N C I L

Letters used. A (2), C (4), D (1), E (2), H (1), I (2), L (1), N (3), O (2), S (1),T (2), U (1),V (1)

Tidbit. Pope John XXIII, elected in 1958, called for a worldwide ecumenical council to help bring the church into the modern world. The church had not seen any significant renewal since the Council of Trent in the 1500s. The Second Vatican Council began in 1962 and lasted until 1965. (Pope John XXIII never saw it completed, because he died in 1963.) The council renewed the liturgy, mandated that it could be said in the congregation's native tongue instead of Latin, turned the priest around to face the people, and allowed for the community's full participation through lay ministry roles.

4. *Answer.* T H E   C O N V E R S I O N   O F
S A U L

Letters used. A (1), C (1), E (2), F (1), H (1), I (1), L (1), N (2), O (3), R (1), S (2), T (1), U (1), V (1)

Tidbit. Saul was a vicious persecutor of the early church until he experienced a conversion while on a journey to Damascus. After being blind for three days, he was healed by Ananias, a Christian sent by Jesus. After his healing, he was baptized by Ananias and began going by his Roman name, Paul. Paul became the greatest missionary the church has ever seen, and he and Peter were the first leaders of the early church.

5. *Answer.* T H E   F I R S T   C O U N C I L   O F
N I C A E A

Letters used. A (2), C (3), E (2), F (2), H (1), I (3), L (1), N (2), O (2), R (1), S (1), T (2), U (1)

Tidbit. This ecumenical council, called by Constantine in 325, assembled more than three hundred bishops to discuss the divinity and humanity of Jesus. The outcome of the council is summed up in the Nicene Creed, which Christians still profess today and which evolved from the original Nicene Creed developed by the council.

Category: Church Life

1. *Answer.* T H E   L I T U R G I C A L   Y E A R
Letters used. A (2), C (1), E (2), G (1), H (1), I (2), L (2), R (2), T (2), U (1), Y (1)

Tidbit. The Catholic church's liturgical year begins with the first Sunday of Advent and concludes on Christ the King Sunday (normally around the end of November). Each year focuses on a particular set of readings, called a cycle, of which there are three. Each cycle highlights a different Gospel, with Cycle A focusing on Matthew, Cycle B on Mark and some of John, and Cycle C on Luke.

2. *Answer.* T H E S T A T I O N S O F T H E C R O S S

Letters used. A (1), C (1), E (2), F (1), H (2), I (1), N (1), O (3), R (1), S (4), T (4)

Tidbit. There are fourteen traditional stations of the cross, each one symbolizing key moments in the Crucifixion of Jesus, beginning with his being sentenced to death and concluding with his body's being placed in the tomb. Most Catholic churches have pictures or carvings of the stations along the interior walls or outside. The stations are often prayerfully remembered or acted out during Lent, especially on Good Friday.

3. *Answer.* T H E L I T U R G Y O F T H E W O R D

Letters used. D (1), E (2), F (1), G (1), H (2), I (1), L (1), O (2), R (2), T (3), U (1), W (1), Y (1)

Tidbit. During the liturgy of the word in Sunday celebrations, the faithful listen to the word of God proclaimed in the Old Testament (first reading), in a psalm (psalm response), and in the New Testament (second reading and Gospel reading). These readings are followed by the homily, in which the presider breaks open the word of God and relates it to the life of the faithful. The saying of the creed and the praying of the general intercessions conclude the liturgy of the word.

4. *Answer.* T H E P A S C H A L C A N D L E

Letters used. A (3), C (2), D (1), E (2), H (2), L (2), N (1), P (1), S (1), T (1)

Tidbit. The paschal candle, or Christ candle, is a large candle that is carried during the processional and is first lit during the Easter Vigil on Holy Saturday. The candle continues to be lit throughout the Easter season and during special sacramental celebrations such as Baptism, Confirmation, and funeral liturgies. The paschal mystery (that Jesus lived, died, and rose again) is the foundation of the Catholic faith, and the candle reminds the faithful of that. The candle is decorated with a cross, the Greek letters *alpha* and *omega,* and the numerals for the current year. A new candle is brought in each year at the Easter Vigil.

5. *Answer.* H O L Y D A Y S O F O B L I G A T I O N

Letters used. A (2), B (1), D (1), F (1), G (1), H (1), I (2), L (2), N (1), O (4), S (1), T (1), Y (2)

Tidbit. Holy days of obligation are special feasts that honor or highlight aspects of the Catholic faith. These days are celebrated by the faithful and usually fall on days other than Sunday. The U.S. bishops have set six:

- Immaculate Conception (8 December)
- Christmas Day (25 December)
- Mary, Mother of God (1 January)
- Ascension (forty days after Easter)
- Assumption (15 August)
- All Saints' Day (1 November)

Category: Who's Who

1. *Answer.* S A I N T F R A N C I S O F A S S I S I

Letters used. A (3), C (1), F (2), I (4), N (2), O (1), R (1), S (5), T (1)

Tidbit. Francis of Assisi (1182–1226) founded the Franciscan order. He spent much of his life avoiding responsibility as the carefree wealthy son of a clothing merchant. After experiencing a couple of visions of Jesus Christ, Francis rejected his wealth and status and gave everything away. From that point on, he lived simply and preached powerfully to all he encountered.

2. *Answer.* P O P E   G R E G O R Y   T H E
       G R E A T

    Letters used. A (1), E (4), G (3), H (1), O (2), P (2), R (3), T (2), Y (1)

    Tidbit. Originally known as Pope Gregory I (about 540–604), Gregory the Great began his political career as the prefect of Rome, which meant he served as governor, chief justice, and chief of police. He finally gave up that life and became a monk, and was elected pope in 590. Gregory became a friend of the poor, an educator of priests and laity alike, and an innovative liturgical musician, introducing what is today known as the Gregorian chant. Gregory's leadership helped bring the church together during a time of tension, especially in Western Europe.

3. *Answer.* S A I N T   T E R E S A   O F   Á V I L A

    Letters used. A (4), E (2), F (1), I (2), L (1), N (1), O (1), R (1), S (2), T (2), V (1)

    Tidbit. Saint Teresa was a Carmelite nun and a great spiritual leader of the church who lived in Spain from 1515 to 1582. After twenty-five years in a huge Carmelite convent, she began her own convent in Ávila, Spain. Her new convent focused on prayer, meditation, and simple living. It became a model for other convents, and Teresa spent much of her time helping to reform convents all over the country. Her writings, especially her book *The Interior Castle,* have provided many people with insights into how to serve God through prayer and love.

4. *Answer.* S A I N T   I G N A T I U S   O F
       L O Y O L A

Letters used. A (3), F (1), G (1), I (3), L (2), N (2), O (3), S (2), T (2), U (1), Y (1)

Tidbit. Ignatius of Loyola (1491–1556) founded the Society of Jesus, also referred to as the Jesuits. While recovering from a war wound, Ignatius began reading many stories of the saints, which prompted him to make a difficult pilgrimage to Rome. After that journey, he became a priest. Ignatius created a process, known as the Spiritual Exercises, that can lead people to a deeper relationship with Jesus Christ. Because of the emphasis he placed on education, many of his followers found themselves teaching at the major universities in the Catholic areas of Europe and soon were running seminaries and colleges and schools throughout the world.

5. *Answer.* O U R   L A D Y   O F
G U A D A L U P E

Letters used. A (3), D (2), E (1), F (1), G (1), L (2), O (2), P (1), R (1), U (3), Y (1)

Tidbit. In 1531, a young Aztec peasant named Juan Diego encountered a vision of the Virgin Mary on a hillside in Mexico. The Virgin appeared to Juan as an Aztec, and spoke his language. She instructed Juan to go to the bishop of Mexico City and ask him to build a temple on the hillside. The bishop did not believe Juan and sent him away. Mary appeared to Juan again, and this time instructed him to gather some roses that were growing out of season, wrap them in his cloak, and bring them to the bishop as proof that he had seen her. Juan did as he was told. When he opened his cloak to show the bishop the roses, a brightly colored image of the Virgin Mary was imprinted on the cloak, and it convinced the bishop that Juan had seen the Virgin. Juan's cloak has been preserved to this day, and the image on it remains as bright and clear as ever. Our Lady of Guadalupe is one of the most recognizable images in the Latin American church.

GRACE BALL

Object of the Game

This game is modeled after the game baseball. The group is divided into two opposing teams, and the group leader acts as the pitcher for both sides. The pitcher "throws" a question at each "batter." Each correct answer is treated as a base hit, and each incorrect response as an out. Runs and innings are scored according to the regular rules of baseball, with the pitcher throwing an occasional "home run" or "extra base hit" to give the team at bat a chance to clear the bases or score extra runs.

HOW THE GAME IS PLAYED

Players

☐ one pitcher (the group leader)
☐ two teams (each comprising half of the group)
☐ one scorekeeper

Supplies

☐ a scoreboard (see the scoreboard setup instructions on page 122)
☐ prizes (optional)

Room Setup

Set up the room according to the diagram below, using chairs or corners of the room to designate home plate, first base, and so on.

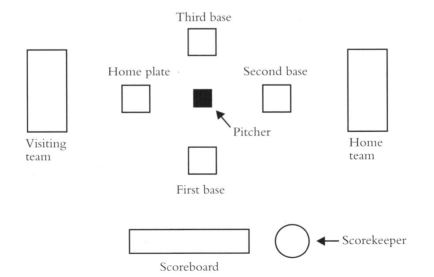

Scoreboard Setup

Provide materials so that the scorekeeper can create the following scoreboard on a chalkboard or overhead transparency. The markings shown should be permanent, and the outs and runs should be erasable so that the scorekeeper can update them as necessary.

Game Directions

1. The group leader selects one person to be the scorekeeper and asks that person to set up the scoreboard as shown in the preceding section. The leader divides the remainder of the group into two teams, and assigns one person to be the "coach" of each team. The leader explains that this person is to establish the team's "batting order," that is, the order in which the people on the team will go to "bat" by answering a question "thrown" to them by the "pitcher" (the group leader). The leader encourages each team to develop a name connected to Catholic identity, such as the Charitable Givers, the Saints, or the Jesuits.

2. The pitcher flips a coin to see what order the teams bat in. The team winning the toss is designated the visiting team and bats first. The visiting team sits behind home plate, and the home team sits in the field.

3. The first batter steps up to home plate, and the pitcher asks a question from the questions-and-answers section on pages 125–135. Only the batter may answer the question. If the batter gives an incorrect answer or a teammate offers an answer or a hint, the batter is

counted out and the next batter is up. If the batter gives the correct answer, it is counted as a hit, and the batter moves to first base. The play continues with new batters until the team collects three outs. With each hit, the batter moves to first base, and any players on base move forward one base. Every time a player moves to home plate, the team scores a run.

4. Some of the "Grace Ball" questions are marked with an asterisk. These are home run questions. If they are answered correctly, the batter and everyone on base moves to home plate, all scoring runs. If the batter answers incorrectly, the batter is counted out.

5. Some of the "Grace Ball" questions are accompanied by an extra base hit question. This follow-up question is asked if the batter answers the initial question correctly, and is answered by the same batter who answered the initial question. If the extra base hit question is answered correctly, then everyone on base moves ahead an additional base, for a total of two bases. If the extra question is answered incorrectly, no out is recorded and those on base stay where they are, having already gained one base for the initial question that was answered correctly.

6. After three outs, the batting team's half of the inning is over, and the teams change sides.

7. The scorekeeper keeps track of the outs and total runs for each inning. When time is up or the teams have finished seven innings, the team with the most runs is declared the winner.

Variations on the Game

Team-developed questions. Instead of acting as pitcher and using the questions provided, direct the teams to develop their own questions and answers. Play the game as directed, except invite the members of the nonbatting team to take turns pitching the questions to the batters. This works best if an assigned topic (such as sacraments or prayers) is used to help narrow the field of questions and keep them applicable to what the young people are learning or reviewing.

Test or review. This game can be adapted for a test or for a chapter review. If the teacher's manual contains sample test questions, they can easily be used as the questions the pitcher throws to the batter.

Tournament. If you have a large group, divide it into four or more teams and sponsor a tournament in which the teams play one another over the course of a few days or several weeks. Offer the team with the best record a group prize or award.

GRACE BALL—QUESTIONS AND ANSWERS

An asterisk (★) indicates a home run question.

 Extra base hit questions *do not* count as outs if they are answered incorrectly. If they are answered correctly, every person on base moves ahead an extra base.

1. Recite the Glory to the Father.
 Answer.
Glory to the Father, and to the Son,
  and to the Holy Spirit:
As it was in the beginning, is now,
  and will be for ever.
Amen.

2. What is a shrine?
 Answer. A shrine is a place designated by the church as significant, because of an approved miraculous phenomenon. Many shrines have become destinations for pilgrimages.

3. Where are the letters *INRI* usually found?
 Answer. above the figure of Jesus on a crucifix

★4. Where do the ashes used for Ash Wednesday come from?
 Answer. the burned palms from the previous year's Palm Sunday

5. What is a novena?
 Answer. A novena is a devotion consisting of nine straight days of prayer for a special intention. The novena originated from the nine days of prayer by the Apostles and Mary between Ascension and Pentecost.

6. How many sacraments does the Catholic church celebrate?
 Answer. seven
 Extra base hit question. Name them.
 Extra base hit answer. Anointing of the Sick, Baptism, Confirmation, the Eucharist, Holy Orders, Matrimony, and Reconciliation

7. What do we call the blessed oil that is used to anoint people for Baptism or Confirmation?

Answer. We call it chrism. The oil is traditionally blessed on Holy Thursday by a bishop at a cathedral.

8. What does the word *amen* mean?

Answer. Amen means "I believe," "It is true," or "So be it." The word signifies a commitment to what has been spoken.

★9. What does the lectionary contain?

Answer. The lectionary is a collection of Scripture readings proclaimed at each weekday and Sunday Mass.

10. What is a chasuble?

Answer. A chasuble is the external garment worn by the presider at the Eucharist.

11. The altar is located in which part of the church?

Answer. the sanctuary, which also contains the pulpit and the presider's chair

12. Where is the consecrated host kept?

Answer. in the tabernacle, which is a secure place for reserving and worshiping the Blessed Sacrament

★13. What type of candles are usually found on a side altar?

Answer. votive, or vigil, candles

14. The cloth used to clean the sacred vessels after Communion is called the what?

Answer. purificator

15. What is the candle near the tabernacle called?

Answer. It is called the sanctuary lamp, and it signals the presence of the Blessed Sacrament.

16. Name two of the three ways that sacred materials (such as consecrated wine or bread) can be disposed of.

Answer. They may be burned, buried, or consumed.

17. A pyx (pronounced "pic") is used to carry what?

Answer. This container is used to carry the consecrated Communion host outside of church and Mass.

18. The large candle that is lit during the Easter season and for other special occasions, such as Baptism, is called what?

Answer. It is called the paschal candle. It is also known as the Christ candle.

★19. What is the name of the book used by the priest that contains the prayers said at Mass?

Answer. the sacramentary

20. Where might you find an alb in a church?

Answer. You would find it on a priest or deacon. This long, loose-fitting tunic is worn under other vestments, and is common to all ministers in worship.

21. Name the two most significant liturgical celebrations for Catholics.

Answer. Easter and Christmas

Extra base hit question. Name the seasons of preparation that precede them.

Extra base hit answer. Advent before Christmas, and Lent before Easter

22. How many weeks does Advent last?

Answer. The season of expectation of Christ lasts four weeks.

23. Pentecost celebrates what historical event?

Answer. the Holy Spirit's descending upon the disciples and the beginning (or "birthday") of the church

★24. What feast is celebrated on the last Sunday of the liturgical year?
Answer. Christ the King

25. What liturgical season uses the color green?
Answer. Ordinary Time uses green. The color symbolizes hope, growth, life, and fidelity.

26. What day begins the observance of Lent?
Answer. Ash Wednesday

27. What differentiates the liturgical cycles (A, B, and C) from one another?
Answer. Different Gospels and Scripture readings are highlighted or used with each cycle. Primarily, the Gospel of Matthew is proclaimed in Cycle A, the Gospels of Mark and John in Cycle B, and the Gospel of Luke in Cycle C.

★28. When does the Triduum season occur?
Answer. during Holy Week, right before Easter
Extra base hit question. Name the days that make up the Triduum.
Extra base hit answer. Holy Thursday, Good Friday, Holy Saturday, and Easter Sunday

29. What liturgical season follows Advent?
Answer. the Christmas season

30. A monstrance holds what?
Answer. a consecrated host that is used for devotions such as the Benediction

31. What are the two main parts of the Mass?
Answer. the liturgy of the word and the liturgy of the Eucharist

32. The Kyrie Eleison is also known as what?
Answer. the Lord, Have Mercy, or the penitential rite

33. What part of the Scriptures is heard during the second reading at Mass?

Answer. any part of the New Testament other than the Gospels

34. The consecration occurs during which major part of the Mass?

Answer. the liturgy of the Eucharist

35. What is a ciborium?

Answer. A ciborium is a container for the Communion host. It resembles a chalice except that it has a cover.

★**36.** What is a processional cross?

Answer. a mobile cross or crucifix that leads the procession and recession of liturgical ministers

37. What part of the Scriptures is usually heard during the first reading?

Answer. the Old Testament

38. What part of the Scriptures is usually sung at Mass?

Answer. A psalm is usually sung between the first and second readings.

39. What is the difference between a stole worn by a priest and one worn by a deacon at Mass?

Answer. A priest wears his stole vertically, whereas a deacon wears his over one shoulder at an angle.

40. What is the name of the cloth that is placed on the altar, under the chalice and paten?

Answer. the corporal

★**41.** How many decades are found on a rosary?

Answer. five

42. How many times a day do church bells ring to remind people to pray the Angelus?

Answer. three (at 6 a.m., noon, and 6 p.m.)

43. When is an Act of Contrition usually said?

Answer. during the sacrament of Reconciliation, after the confession of sins

44. How many stations make up the traditional stations of the cross?

Answer. fourteen

45. What happens at the Benediction?

Answer. The Blessed Sacrament is placed in a monstrance, prayers are offered, and the people are blessed.

★46. A 40-hour adoration involves what?

Answer. This involves prayer before the Blessed Sacrament for 40 hours in a row. It is usually done in shifts with a number of people.

47. Morning and evening prayer are part of what prayer form?

Answer. They are part of the liturgy of the hours, formerly called the Divine Office. This is the church's full cycle of daily prayer.

48. What does the term *Eucharist* mean?

Answer. "to give thanks or thanksgiving"

49. The Immaculate Conception celebrates what?

Answer. Mary's being conceived without original sin

Extra base hit question. Name the date this feast is celebrated.

Extra base hit answer. 8 December

★50. A saint's feast day is usually the same day as what?

Answer. the anniversary of the saint's death

51. Name the four Gospels in the order in which they appear in the New Testament.

Answer. Matthew, Mark, Luke, and John

52. Which is the oldest and most important feast day of Mary?

Answer. the solemnity of Mary, Mother of God, celebrated on 1 January each year

53. During what time period did the Crusades occur?
Answer. the Middle Ages

54. Name the three synoptic Gospels.
Answer. Matthew, Mark, and Luke
Extra base hit question. What does *synoptic* mean?
Extra base hit answer. "similar in style and sharing much of the same content" (from the Greek word that means "seeing the whole together")

55. The process of a person's officially becoming a saint is known as what?
Answer. canonization

*56. Who began the Reformation?
Answer. Martin Luther began the Reformation when he sent his Ninety-five Theses to the church of Wittenberg, outlining abuses committed by the church, including the selling of indulgences.

57. Which was the first Gospel to be written?
Answer. Mark

58. Which month is commonly known for its many Marian celebrations and crownings?
Answer. May

59. Which pope introduced Vatican Council II?
Answer. Pope John XXIII
Extra base hit question. Which pope brought Vatican Council II to a conclusion?
Extra base hit answer. Pope Paul VI

60. Who prepared the way for Jesus' ministry by preaching repentance of sins?
Answer. John thess Baptist

★61. What is a sacramental seal?

Answer. the priest's obligation of secrecy in the sacrament of Reconciliation; sometimes called the seal of the confession

62. What was the split between the Eastern church and the Western church called?

Answer. the Great Schism (1054)

63. Which was the last Gospel to be written?

Answer. John

64. Who sentenced Jesus to death?

Answer. Pontius Pilate

★65. Name the four marks of the church.

Answer. one, holy, catholic, and apostolic

66. Who is known as the first martyr for his faith?

Answer. Stephen, who was stoned to death for professing his faith in Jesus

67. Which book in the Scriptures outlines the life of the early church?

Answer. Acts of the Apostles

68. What is a litany?

Answer. a prayer consisting of a series of supplications and responses said alternately by a leader and a group

69. Who is the patron saint of hopeless or impossible causes?

Answer. Saint Jude

70. What city was Jesus born in?

Answer. Bethlehem

71. Who serves as the bishop of Rome?

Answer. the pope

72. What was Jesus' hometown?
Answer. Nazareth

★73. In art, what usually distinguishes someone as a saint?
Answer. a halo

74. What color is often associated with Mary?
Answer. blue

75. Whose conversion resulted in the acceptance of Christianity as the official religion of the Roman Empire?
Answer. Emperor Constantine's

76. How many years did Jesus' public ministry last?
Answer. three

77. Which feast celebrates the announcement of the Incarnation to Mary?
Answer. the Annunciation

78. Who was the first person to discover the empty tomb of Jesus?
Answer. Mary Magdalene

79. What statement came out of the First Council of Nicaea?
Answer. the original Nicene Creed

★80. What is an encyclical?
Answer. a letter to the universal church, usually doctrinal, written by the pope

81. Who wrote the Acts of the Apostles?
Answer. Luke

82. The feast of the Visitation celebrates Mary's visit with whom?
Answer. her cousin Elizabeth
Extra base hit question. What child was Elizabeth pregnant with?
Extra base hit answer. John the Baptist

83. Finish this saying: "Blessed are the poor in spirit . . ."
Answer. "for theirs is the kingdom of heaven" (Matthew 5:3).

84. Recite the first two sentences of the Nicene Creed.
Answer.
We believe in one God,
    the Father, the Almighty,
    maker of heaven and earth,
    of all that is, seen and unseen.

We believe in one Lord, Jesus Christ,
    the only Son of God
    eternally begotten of the Father,
    God from God, Light from Light,
    true God from true God,
    begotten, not made, one in Being with the Father.

★85. What is the difference between a permanent deacon and a transitional one?
Answer. A permanent deacon can be married, whereas a transitional deacon cannot because his office is a step toward priestly ordination.

86. What is the New Testament book of apocalyptic literature called?
Answer. Revelation

87. What is a novena?
Answer. a prayer with a specific intention, offered nine days in a row

88. Who serves as the head of a diocese?
Answer. a bishop, an archbishop, or a cardinal

89. What feast celebrates the saints as a group?
Answer. All Saints' Day
Extra base hit question. Name the date it is held each year.
Extra base hit answer. 1 November

90. Who is known as the Beloved Disciple?
Answer. John

91. Who began the Episcopal church?
Answer. King Henry VIII of England

92. Which Gospel is the shortest?
Answer. Mark

93. What is the name of the song that Mary sang during her visit with Elizabeth?
Answer. the Magnificat

★94. What special role does the College of Cardinals have?
Answer. to elect a new pope

95. What does the term *ecumenism* mean?
Answer. "the effort to foster unity among all Christian denominations, particularly between Catholics and Protestants"

96. Name the five basic forms of prayer.
Answer. blessing, intercession, petition, praise, and thanksgiving

97. What feast is often called the birthday of the church?
Answer. Pentecost
Extra base hit question. How many days after Easter is it celebrated?
Extra base hit answer. fifty (hence, *pente-*)

98. Which will you usually see in a Protestant church—a cross or a crucifix?
Answer. a cross

99. What is the name of the governing agency of the Vatican?
Answer. the Roman curia

★100. Whose version of the Bible contains more books—Catholics' or Protestants'?
Answer. Catholics'. Catholic Bibles contain seventy-three books and letters—seven more than are found in Protestant versions.

CATHOLIC PICTIONARY

Object of the Game

This game is similar to the board game *Pictionary.* In this version, the group is divided into teams. A member of each team is given a word or phrase that describes a Catholic person, event, sacramental, or prayer, and asked to draw it. The other members of each team must guess what is being drawn in the allotted time.

HOW THE GAME IS PLAYED

Players

☐ two to four teams of at least two people each
☐ one leader, who also is the scorekeeper

Supplies

☐ a separate easel and newsprint for each team, or a chalkboard big enough so that each team has a section to draw on
☐ markers or chalk
☐ a watch or clock that displays seconds
☐ one die
☐ words-and-phrases cards cut from a copy of pages 140–142, or slips of paper and a pencil for writing the words and phrases
☐ prizes (optional)

Game Directions

1. The leader divides the group into two to four teams of at least two players each. (Playing with more than four teams at a time is not recommended.) Each team must decide the order in which its members will take a turn drawing. Every member of a team must take a turn drawing before any member draws again.

2. The leader invites to go first the team with the member who possesses the longest last name. The leader asks someone from the team to roll the die. If an even number comes up, the round is considered an all-play round (indicated by an asterisk on pages 140–142), which means that simultaneously, one person from each team will draw and all the teams will try to guess what is being drawn. If an odd number comes up on the die, only the person who rolled the die gets to draw, and only that person's team is allowed to call out guesses. Each number on the die corresponds to a particular "Catholic Pictionary" category, as follows:

If the Die Reads . . .	*The Category Is . . .*
1	"Saints and Leaders"
★2	"Historical Events"
3	"Who's Who"
★4	"Liturgical Objects"
5	"Catholic Prayers"
★6	"Feasts and Holy Days"

An asterisk (★) indicates an all-play category.

3. The leader locates the category in the words-and-phrases section on pages 140–142 and picks a word or phrase from that category. The leader then shows a card displaying that word or phrase to the person or persons drawing, or writes the word or phrase on a slip of paper and shows the slip of paper to those drawing. When they are ready, the leader gives the signal to begin drawing.

4. Those who are drawing must remain silent and cannot draw letters or numbers. If a team member correctly guesses a part of the word or phrase, the person or persons drawing may write that part on the newsprint or board and even draw one or more lines before or after it to indicate where it fits in the complete answer. For example, if the phrase being drawn is "Holy Week," and someone in the group guesses "Holy," the person drawing may write on the board, "Holy _____."

5. Those who are drawing are given 2 minutes to illustrate their event, prayer, person, or object. The leader must listen very carefully for the first person to correctly guess the answer. If a form of the answer is given, but the guess is not exactly right, the leader should wait until someone says the exact answer. At that point, the leader stops the drawing, checks the time, and awards points to the team with the correct answer. If the correct answer is not given within 2 minutes, no points are scored. Scoring is as follows:

- Correct answer in an all-play round: 10 points
- Correct answer in a single-play round: 5 points
- Incorrect or no answer in any round: 0 points

6. After a word or phrase is guessed correctly, the leader invites the players to share what they know about the event, prayer, person, or object. If a word or phrase is not guessed, the leader offers hints to help the group guess the correct answer.

7. The opportunity to roll the die and play alone continues in a clockwise fashion through all the teams. This is true even if an even number is rolled, indicating an all-play round. No matter which team answers the all-play round correctly, the team that goes next is the one to the left of the team that rolled the die for that round.

8. The leader keeps track of each team's score. After the allotted time or number of rounds, the leader declares the team with the highest score the winner and passes out prizes if they are being used.

Variations on the Game

Single player. Instead of playing team against team, invite group members to the newsprint or board one at a time and show them the word or phrase. Have the person at the newsprint or board draw the word or phrase until the group guesses it correctly. Record times and see who can guess the fastest.

"Reverse Catholic Pictionary." Invite one or more people to go to the newsprint or board to do the drawing. While their backs are turned, show the rest of the group the word or phrase. Then encourage the group to use shapes and sizes and directions to guide the people who are drawing, until those people can guess what the word or phrase is. Tell those describing the word or phrase that they cannot use any part of the actual word or phrase.

CATHOLIC PICTIONARY—WORDS AND PHRASES

Category One: Saints and Leaders

Saint Thérèse of Lisieux ("the Little Flower")	Saint Thomas ("Doubting Thomas")
Pope John Paul II	Saint Joan of Arc
Saint Stephen (the first martyr)	Saint Patrick
Saint Francis of Assisi	Saint Mary
Mother Teresa of Calcutta	Saint Joseph the Worker

*Category Two: Historical Events

Pentecost	the Great Schism
the Crusades	the Council of Trent
the Middle Ages	the Counter-Reformation
the Protestant Reformation	the Edict of Milan
Vatican Council II	the Enlightenment

Permission to reproduce this page for program use is granted.

Category Three: Who's Who

youth minister	music minister
pope	priest
deacon	lector
cardinal	bishop
sister	director of religious education

*Category Four: Liturgical Objects

alb	paschal candle
chalice	altar
tabernacle	crucifix
stole	baptismal font
lectionary	stations of the cross

Category Five: Catholic Prayers

sign of the cross	Gloria
Hail Mary	Magnificat
Kyrie Eleison	rosary
Act of Contrition	Glory Be to the Father
Lord's Prayer	Lamb of God

*Category Six: Feasts and Holy Days

the Immaculate Conception	Christ the King Sunday
Ash Wednesday	Holy Family
Palm Sunday	Christmas
Easter Sunday	All Saints' Day
All Souls' Day	Good Friday

Permission to reproduce this page for program use is granted.

Acknowedgments *(continued from copyright page)*

The scriptural quotations contained herein are from the New Revised Standard Version of the Bible. Copyright © 1989 by the Division of Christian Education of the National Council of the Churches of Christ in the United States of America. All rights reserved.

The words of the Hail Mary on page 95 and of the Glory to the Father on pages 95 and 125 are quoted from *Catholic Household Blessings and Prayers,* by the Bishop's Committee on the Liturgy and the National Conference of Catholic Bishops (Washington: United States Catholic Conference, 1988), pages 363 and 391. Copyright © 1988 by the United States Conference of Catholic Bishops (USCCB).

The Final Doxology on page 95 is quoted from *The Roman Missal,* English translation prepared by the International Commission on English in the Liturgy (New York: Catholic Book Publishing Co., 1987), page 551. Illustrations and arrangement copyright © 1985–1974 by Catholic Book Publishing Co., New York. All rights reserved. Used with permission.

The words of the Nicene Creed on pages 95 and 134 and of the Lord's Prayer on pages 95 and 96 are quoted from the *Catechism of the Catholic Church* for the United States of America, second edition, page 49 and number 2759. Copyright © 1994 by the USCCB—Libreria Editrice Vaticana. English translation of the *Catechism of the Catholic Church: Modifications from the Editio Typica* copyright © 1997 by the USCCB—Libreria Editrice Vaticana.

The words of the Confiteor and the Glory to God on pages 95 and 96 are quoted from *Today's Missal,* volume 68, number 6, pages 8 and 11. Copyright © 2001 by Oregon Catholic Press.

READY-TO-GO GAME SHOWS (THAT TEACH SERIOUS STUFF): BIBLE EDITION

by Michael Theisen

The Bible edition of *Ready-to-Go Game Shows* uses interactive game shows similar to the ones familiar to most young people, to grab their attention and increase their biblical knowledge. All the shows can be presented easily, with minimal setup and few required materials. Just add young people, mix, and bake with high energy for a treat worth talking about. Best of all, each show has been field-tested with real teens! The following game shows are included:

- "Who Wants to Be a Bible Millionaire"
- "Faithful Feud"
- "Bible Jeopardy"
- "Holy Word Squares"
- "The Bible Is Right"
- "The Real Fortune"
- "Bible Baseball"
- "Scriptionary"

The fun and popular game ideas in this book will help teachers, youth ministers, and parents reach the maximum learning potential with the young people in their life. (-689-7), 6 x 9, 128 pages, spiral, $19.95

Available from Saint Mary's Press

postal address: 702 Terrace Heights, Winona, MN 55987-1318
toll-free phone number: 800-533-8095
toll-free fax number: 800-344-9225
Web site: www.smp.org
e-mail address: smpress@smp.org